ELECTRIC RIVERS

ELECTRIC RIVERS

The Story of the James Bay Project

Sean McCutcheon

BLACK ROSE BOOKS

Montréal/New York

BLACK ROSE BOOKS No. V169
Hardcover ISBN: 1-895431-19-0
Paperback ISBN: 1-895431-18-2

Canadian Cataloguing in Publication Data

McCutcheon, Sean
   Electric rivers

ISBN: 1-895431-19-0 (bound) – ISBN: 1-895431-18-2

1. James Bay Hydro Electric Project. 2. Indians of North America—James Bay Region (Ont. and Quebec). 3. Inuit—Quebec (Province). 4. Cree Indians—Government relations. I. Title.

FC2925.9.J3M33   1991   333.91′4′0971411   C91-090494-4
F1053.2.M33 1991

Library of Congress Catalog No. 91-72981

Cover Design: Werner Arnold
Maps: *Sémio*Design
Cover Photograph: *Great Whale River,* Hydro Québec
Design and Photocomposition: Nathalie Klym

Editorial Offices
BLACK ROSE BOOKS
3981 St-Laurent Boulevard,
Suite 444
Montréal, Québec
H2W 1Y5 Canada

Mailing Address
BLACK ROSE BOOKS
P.O. Box 1258
Succ. Place du Parc
Montréal, Québec
H2W 2R3 Canada

BLACK ROSE BOOKS
340 Nagel Drive
Cheektowaga, New York
14225 USA

For my parents

Acknowledgements

I have borrowed many of the ideas in this book, and indicate my main sources in its notes and bibliography. For generously sharing information, I particularly wish to thank Harvey Feit, Jacques Guevremont, Walter Hughboy, Kenneth Hare, Carol Karamessines, Hélène Lajambe, Alan Penn, Einar Skinnarland, John Spence, and Jeffrey Wollock. Any errors, of fact or judgement, are mine.

I am grateful to the Canada Council for its support, and grateful above all to Sally Campbell, my editor.

Contents

The James Bay Project

HUDSON BAY

Fort McKenzie

Nastapoca

Caniapisc

Kuujjuarapik /
Whapmagoostui

Great Whale

Great Whale Complex

Caniapiscau

Chisasibi

LG-4

LG-2

LG-3

La Grande

Wemindji

La Grande Complex

Eastmain

Opinaca

Eastmain

JAMES
BAY

Waskaganish

Rupert

Broadback

Mistissini

**Nottaway-
Broadback-
Rupert
(NBR)
Complex**

Harricana

Nottaway

Matagami

0   300 km

The Quebec-Labrador Peninsula

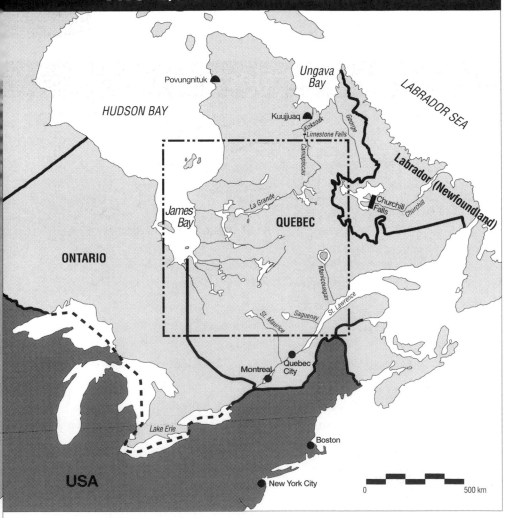

- ◗ Inuit village
- ▲ Cree village

- ▌ Powerhouse, completed
- ▐ Powerhouse, under construction
- ▯ Powerhouse, proposed

Chronology of the James Bay Project

April 1944	Quebec expropriates two privately-owned companies that supplied electricity to Montreal, and gives their assets to a newly-created, publicly-owned utility, Hydro-Québec.
May 1963	Hydro-Québec takes over most of the remaining private power companies and cooperatives in Quebec.
April 1970	Robert Bourassa is elected Premier of Quebec after promising to develop hydroelectric power in the James Bay region.
April 1971	Premier Robert Bourassa launches the James Bay hydroelectric project, a vaguely defined plan to harness some 20 rivers flowing into the eastern side of James and Hudson Bays.
June 1971	Construction crews begin building a road north into the James Bay territory.
April 1972	The Crees and Inuit start court actions to stop the project.
May 1972	The developers announce that the James Bay project will begin with the harnessing of the La Grande River.
December 1972	Hearings begin before Judge Albert Malouf of the Quebec Superior Court on the Native peoples' plea for an injunction.
November 1973	Judge Albert Malouf orders work on the La Grande complex to stop. One week later, after appeal by the developers, his order is reversed.

March 1974	Workers pillage the La Grande-2 construction camp.
August 1974	The Grand Council of the Crees (of Québec) is formed, with Billy Diamond as Grand Chief.
November 1975	The Crees and many of the Inuit sign the James Bay and Northern Québec Agreement with the governments of Canada and Quebec, and with Hydro-Québec and its subsidiaries.
November 1976	René Lévesque's Parti Québécois defeats Robert Bourassa's Liberal party and forms a strongly nationalist government.
October 1979	Inauguration of the La Grande-2 powerhouse.
May 1980	Quebecers vote in a referendum not to give the Parti Québécois government permission to negotiate separation from Canada.
June 1983	The government of Quebec broadens Hydro-Québec's mandate, allowing it to export power under long term contracts.
September 1984	Ten thousand caribou drown while crossing the Caniapiscau River.
December 1985	Phase I of the La Grande complex is completed. The Liberals, led by Robert Bourassa, win a landslide victory over the Parti Québécois. Bourassa, who during the campaign proposed expanding the James Bay project, becomes Premier of Quebec.
March 1988	Bourassa announces that construction would begin in spring 1989 of the second phase of the La Grande complex.
January 1989	The Public Utilities Commission of the State of Maine denies Central Maine Power a permit to import power

from Quebec because the utility has not proven that imports are cheaper than efficiency.

March 1989   Hydro-Québec announces it is reactivating plans to build James Bay II: that is, two new megaprojects in the James Bay and Hudson Bay region, first the Great Whale complex, then the Nottaway-Broadback-Rupert complex.

April 1990   Crees and Inuit take a hybrid canoe/kayak from Great Whale River to New York City to demonstrate their opposition to James Bay II.

September 1991   The New York Power Authority delays for one year ratification of a contract to import 1,000 megawatts of power from Hydro-Québec. Bourassa delays for one year the date at which construction of the Great Whale complex is to begin, until September 1992.

PART ONE

Background

Humans like all other creatures, must make a difference; otherwise, they cannot live…But unlike other creatures, humans must make a choice as to the kind and scale of the difference they make. If they choose to make too small a difference, they diminish their humanity. If they choose to make too great a difference, they diminish nature, and narrow their subsequent choices…

Wendell Berry

Introduction

Like a lobe hanging from an ear, James Bay lies at the southern end of Hudson Bay. These two bays comprise a frigid inland sea, a huge incursion of the Arctic Ocean deep into North America. Between these bays and the Atlantic Ocean lies the Quebec-Labrador Peninsula.

Almost all the people who live on this giant peninsula live in the valley of the Saint Lawrence River, which forms its southern edge. Until the 1970s, though industrial civilization had penetrated and explosively changed most of the rest of the world, the northern half of this peninsula remained the largest area of pristine wilderness in eastern North America, and one of the last large wild parts of the world.

A few adventurers knew of the majestic Torngat mountains, which plunge into the Labrador Sea, or of Ungava Bay, where the tidal range is the greatest in the world, or of the spectacular rivers draining this cold, wet, rocky region. For most of the few city dwellers who even knew it existed, there was nothing in this land but black spruce, stunted in the effort to survive the bitterly cold winters, and barren tundra; plagues of biting flies in summer; and a scattering of the desperately poor Natives who called this desolation home.

In the 1970s, Hydro-Québec, a giant electric utility owned by the government of Quebec, began to divert rivers and flood land, changing forever the James Bay region of this peninsula.

Of the many rivers draining into James Bay and Hudson Bay the largest is named, appropriately, La Grande.[1] From its headwaters in the highlands of the Quebec-Labrador Peninsula, it flows some 800 kilometres westward, down to James Bay. The La Grande is no longer a river. Machines and men have piled up rock, gravel and sand into dams and dikes that divert portions of three other large rivers into the La Grande, and that turn the La Grande into a chain of reservoirs. These rivers have become an engine for generating electricity known as the La Grande complex, phase one.

I climbed once to the crest of the most monumental of all the earthworks built in the James Bay region, the La Grande-2 dam (the second dam counting upstream from the river's mouth, also known as LG-2.) It is as high as a 50-storey building. When I looked downstream, I felt as if I was on top of a mountain. In the valley below I could see roads and a town, power lines swooping away and over the horizon, and sunlight glinting on what remains of the La Grande River as it flowed down to James Bay.

When I turned and looked upstream, I was no longer high but low, on the shore of an artificial lake. The waters of the LG-2 reservoir lapped at my feet, and the far shore was out of sight.

When the dam on which I was standing had first plugged the La Grande the water had started to rise. First it had flooded rivers, streams, and lakes, drowning shorelines where alder and willow had grown, where beaver had built, otters played, and lynx prowled. Then it had climbed the thinly-forested slopes, drowning trees. It took more than a year to fill the reservoir. Of all that was within its perimeter, only the hill tops, now rocky, lichen-splotched, barren islands, are visible.

The water backed up behind the LG-2 dam runs down through tunnels to the mightiest underground powerhouse in the world. There it propels the subtly curved vanes of turbines. The turbines turn. The rotors of the generators mounted above them spin. I have stood within an arm's length of one of these spinning machines as, with an earth-shaking, ear-splitting roar, it transforms the rushing force of what were once mighty rivers into electricity.

From the powerhouses of the La Grande complex a torrent of electricity flows south, through Hydro-Québec's grid of transmission lines and, across the border, through the grid that straddles the northeast of the United States. It mingles with power from other sources. Plugged into this web of power lines are coffee grinders, refrigerators, air conditioners, bulbs and neon tubes, pencil sharpeners, snow-making machinery, televisions, elevators, power tools, aluminum refineries — and, to end a potentially endless list — the computer on which I write these words. As tens of millions of people throughout Quebec and the states of New England and New York turn on and off myriad switches, the energy of sub-Arctic rivers changes, instantly, into light, sound, motion, heat, cold. It is a spectacular trick.

Canada, which is becoming the largest country in the world as the Soviet Union breaks up, has a history of building public works, such as railways, seaways, and pipelines, on a continental scale. But even by Canadian standards, what has been built in the James Bay region is enormous. More than 10,000 square kilometres of natural waterways and land have been flooded. Running at full output, the three power stations of the first phase of the La Grande complex can generate some 10,300 megawatts.[2] To build this complex, the most powerful in North America, and its associated power lines, cost some $16-billion, according to its developers.

Hydro-Québec is now building more powerhouses within the La Grande complex. When this second phase is complete in 1995, the power output of the La Grande complex will have risen to 15,000 megawatts.

Hydro-Québec plans to more build two more hydroelectric complexes which together comprise what is known as James Bay II — a geographically inaccurate name, for the first of these complexes is to be centred on the Great Whale River, which empties into Hudson Bay. The second complex will be on the Nottaway, Broadback, and Rupert rivers, which do flow into James Bay, south of the La Grande.

If Hydro-Québec does complete the James Bay project despite the storm of protest it has aroused, then, by the first decade of the twenty-first century, it will have reduced to servitude every major river flowing from Quebec into James Bay and southern Hudson Bay save one,[3] as well as rivers flowing into Ungava Bay. It will have built dozens of towns, airports and power stations, hundreds of dams and dykes, thousands of kilometres of roads and high voltage power lines. The total area of all the reservoirs created will be about that of Lake Erie. All the water draining a tract of land two-thirds the size of France, half the size of Texas, will be regulated. The entire James Bay project will generate, at peak output, some 27,000 megawatts of power, equivalent to the output of 35 or more nuclear power plants. Hydro-Québec, which now generates a quarter of all the hydroelectricity in North America, will have increased that fraction to two-thirds.

The James Bay project is one of the largest energy projects ever. It is no mere megaproject. "Mega" denotes only a million, but the magnitude of this project is measured in billions of watts and dollars. "Giga" denotes a billion. This is a gigaproject.

When we switch on a light, we do not often wonder where the power comes from, or who decided that the system should be thus, or what the consequences were of this decision. In a habitual gesture as free of thought as breathing, we just flick the switch. But technology, like art, is created. It is a crystallization of scientists' insights and engineers' ingenuity. The James Bay project is a magnificent technological achievement. Technology is also an instrument of politics. In creating wealth and gaining power for some Quebecers, the James Bay project is sweeping away much that makes land and life precious to the Cree Indians of northern Quebec; and in fighting against it, they are gaining power.

This book is about why and how the James Bay project is being built, how it works, the consequences of building it on people and on nature, and the struggle to stop it.

NOTES

1. Four cultural groups — Indians, Inuit, French and English — have settled the Quebec-Labrador Peninsula and named its geographical features and places, some of which, in consequence, have four names. Chisasibi, the Cree name for the La Grande, means great river, as does the French name. The English called this the George River.
2. A watt is the basic unit for measuring electric power, that is, the rate at which electric energy flows. A kilowatt (kW) equals a thousand watts, and a megawatt (MW), the unit in which large flows of power is measured, equals a million watts. A kilowatt-hour (kWh), the common unit for measuring electric energy, is the amount of energy delivered by a power flow of one kilowatt over the course of an hour. The average home in Montreal consumes about 28,000 kilowatthours in a year. Large quantities of electric energy are measures in units of terawatthours (TWh). A terawatthour equals a billion kilowatthours. Montreal — that is, the city on the island of Montreal — consumes between 30 and 40 terawatthours of electricity in a year.
3. No hydroelectric developments are planned for the Harricana River, but it is slated for use in the GRAND Canal water-diversion scheme (described on page 136).

CHAPTER 1

Natural and Human History

I grew up in Dublin, a city which lies at almost the same latitude as Chisasibi, the Cree village at the mouth of the La Grande River. Winters in Dublin are mild enough for boys to wear short pants year round. If kids in Chisasibi were to bare their legs in winter they would lose them. The temperature there, averaged over the year, is below freezing, and often plunges to 40 below in winter.

What makes the Quebec-Labrador Peninsula so cold is the frigid water of Hudson Bay and James Bay. Bodies of water usually moderate climate, but in winter this water is ice-covered, and, with the frozen land around, acts as a vast cold plate chilling the air. (When people in Boston and New York City shiver in winter it is because air masses chilled over this water have swept south.) The water of Hudson Bay and James Bay also makes the Quebec-Labrador Peninsula moist; in fall and early winter the prevailing west winds pick up moisture from these bays and dump it on the eastern slopes of the peninsula. The region east of James Bay has colder temperatures and heavier snow falls than Ireland, or than any other place in the world at comparable latitudes.

The James Bay neighbourhood was the birthplace of the greatest of the glaciers which, during the Ice Age, covered a third of all Earth's lands. Long after the ice elsewhere had melted, it lingered in the Quebec-Labrador Peninsula. When, finally, it melted, water began to drain from the central plateau north to Ungava Bay, through long valleys arranged like spokes of a wheel, south to the Gulf of Saint Lawrence, east to the Labrador Sea, and west to James Bay and Hudson Bay.

The Quebec-Labrador Peninsula is a hydrological phenomenon. It has, per unit of surface area, more running water (and, some say, more beautiful rivers) than almost any other part of the world. This is not so much because a lot of rain and snow falls, but because it is so cold that of the water that does fall, very little evaporates. Much of this water — in fact a third of all the water flowing in Canada's rivers — flows into James Bay and Hudson Bay, which occupy a low basin at the heart of the great sweep of rocks known as the Canadian Shield. So much fresh water enters these bays that they are less salty than the Arctic Ocean, to which they are connected.

Relatively few species of plants or animals can cope with the exacting physical environment of the James Bay region, with its thin, poor soil, and its cold and wide-ranging temperatures.

On the sodden ground which was exposed by the melting ice, a sparse forest dominated by black spruce now grows. The spruce dominate by numbers, not by size: the oldest trees, veterans of more than a hundred winters, are not much taller than a professional basketball player, and no thicker than his thigh. Caribou moss, a pale-green lichen, carpets the ground beneath the dark and spindly trees.

This kind of ecosystem is known as taiga, the Russian name for the great belt of evergreen forest that circles the northern parts of the planet.

The James Bay region is similar to Siberia. The taiga's northern limit here roughly follows the 55th parallel. Farther north, where trees cannot grow, lies tundra. Both taiga and tundra are low energy environments. Here, plants slowly transform solar energy into leaf and stem, and the food they offer other forms of life is spread sparsely over great areas.

Roughly 100 species of birds, 20 species of fish, and 40 species of mammals are robust enough to live in the Quebec taiga. Population densities are low, but the strategies these fauna have for harvesting food are cunning, and the areas they harvest are huge, so their populations can be large. Along the eastern shores of James Bay, millions of gobbling, honking geese have proclaimed the arrival of spring ever since the Ice Age. They, and many other migratory birds, flock to the coastal wetland where they feed and where some also nest. The fish — they include whitefish, pike and salmon — grow gradually but can reach noble age and size; rivers and lakes here are a fisherman's paradise. Of the mammals — they also include beaver, muskrat, lynx, red fox and black bear — the caribou most clearly shows the classic nomadic strategy for coping. It compensates for slim pickings — in winter, especially, when it lives by digging down through snow with its broad hooves for lichen — by migrating continually around the Quebec-Labrador Peninsula. The George River herd is the largest in the world.

Between four and five millennia ago, roughly the era when the Sphinx and the Great Pyramid of Cheops were built, humans moved to northern Quebec. They were Indians, people of the canoe, toboggan and snowshoe, and they traveled along the rivers to occupy the taiga. Of the Indian groups in the Quebec-Labrador Peninsula, the largest is that of the Crees, who hunt waterfowl on the coast of James Bay, and caribou and other game inland. Far inland, in the rugged heart of the Quebec-Labrador Peninsula, live the Naskapi Indians, caribou hunters, and south of them, the Montagnais. These three groups are related; their native tongues all belong to the Algonkian family of Indian languages. Inuit, people of the kayak, igloo, and dog team, came by sea to the tundra. They hunted seal and other marine wildlife in coastal areas, and caribou inland.

Both Indians and Inuit were nomads, moving almost continually to wrest a bare living from thinly-spread resources. They lived on small game, such as rabbits and grouse, on fish, and on caribou, their most-prized quarry. A caribou gave many meals of tasty meat and bone marrow, the most food for the least hunting effort. It also provided, among other things, fat for fueling lamps; antlers for making needles, spear points and harpoons; hides for warm clothing, tough shoes, and weatherproof tent coverings; and tendons and ligaments for tying tent frames.[1] In the 16th century, a second wave of migrants began to settle the Quebec-Labrador Peninsula. Jacques Cartier, looking for a sea route leading northwest to the Orient, sailed along the north shore of the Gulf of Saint Lawrence and was reminded of the barren land to which, according to Genesis, God banished Cain for killing Abel. One of the first Europeans to see the Quebec-Labrador Peninsula, Cartier described it as "the land God gave to Cain."

At the beginning of the 17th century French colonists founded a settlement by the rocky promontory constricting the mighty Saint Lawrence River which Cartier, borrowing the local Indians' name for the site, a name which means "where the river narrows," had called Québec. The Saint Lawrence Valley became the heart of the colony of Nouvelle-France. From New France the French explored half the continent, sprinkling it with French names, and shipping its riches, mostly furs, back to France.

The first of the hairy, pale-skinned strangers the Natives of the James Bay region met were English. In 1610 Henry Hudson rounded the top of the Quebec-Labrador Peninsula and sailed into the bay which bears his name. It was a dead end in two senses: he could find no exit leading west; and his mutinous crew sailed home after a hard winter, leaving Hudson, his son, and seven faithful seamen adrift in a small boat to die. At the end of his last winter, Hudson met an Indian. They exchanged "two beaver skinnes and two deere skinnes" for a knife, mirror, buttons and a hatchet. This is the first recorded contact between Europeans and Natives in the James Bay area.

With the exception of Thomas James, who wintered with his crew in the bay that now bears his name, it was not until 1668 that Europeans returned to James Bay. They were British, again. After wintering and trading in James Bay, they sailed home with enough lustrous pelts to make, in the words of a London newspaper, "some recompense for [their] cold confinement." To the backers of this voyage, a group of merchants and aristocrats who called themselves The Governor and Company of Adventurers of England Trading into Hudson Bay — or, less resonantly, the Hudson's Bay Company — King Charles II airily granted all the lands draining into Hudson Bay, a vast territory they named Rupert's Land.

At the Hudson's Bay Company trading posts the Indians exchanged furs for such useful or comforting products of industrial technology as muskets, ammunition, axes, knives, kettles, blankets, flour, matches, tobacco, tea and brandy. As the fur trade developed, the Crees no longer hunted only for meat; they also trapped beaver and other fur-bearing animals to trade. The fur trade was a partnership between Natives and non-Natives, but an unequal one. The Indians were not dispossessed, for the traders needed them, but they were not paid much. Crees today say that in exchange for a long-barreled musket, their forefathers had to give a stack of pelts as high as the gun was long — and that the traders would weigh down the stack with a rock.

The James Bay region was the hub from which, following rivers, the Hudson's Bay Company expanded to become, for several centuries, the world's greatest commercial empire, a megaproject harvesting resources, and hence wealth, from an immense territory.

New France, meanwhile, the colony which Voltaire had dismissed as "a few acres of snow," as a place "where miserable settlers squatted 'twixt bear and beaver," was lost by France in one of a series of border wars between it and England, its great rival. After a British army defeated a French one on the heights above Quebec City in 1759, New France was merged into British North America. The French elite sailed home after the conquest of New France, leaving 65,000 or so *Canadiens* behind in the Saint Lawrence Valley.

The British conquerors were not particularly cruel by the standards of the time, but neither were they eager to share power with the conquered. In 1837, reporting on the state of British North America after a rebellion by the *Canadiens* had been crushed, "Radical Jack" Durham called the French and the English "two warring nations within the bosom of a single state" and recommended that what he called the French-Canadians, "a people without history and without literature" be assimilated into English culture.

The French-Canadians had a culture, of course. It was marked by resignation and nostalgia: its symbols were the docile lamb, emblem of their patron saint, Saint Jean-Baptiste, and the *fleur de lis* (the white lily), emblem of French royalty, a flower far too delicate to survive a Quebec winter. The French Canadians clung to their language, and remained distinct.

After World War II, Quebec began to industrialize. As people left their farms to work in Montreal and other cities, the traditional authority of the Church eroded. French Canadians saw themselves as an oppressed minority, Canada's blacks, relegated to low-class jobs and salaries. A new generation of nationalists began to articulate the desire for respect and power and independence from Canada. The French-speaking people of Quebec began to called themselves Québécois. In 1960, they elected the provincial Liberal party to power and launched the *Révolution tranquille*, the Quiet Revolution, the transformation of Quebec into a modern, secular state. The provincial government took over from the Church in running hospitals, leisure, culture and communications. It became the principal agent in the economy, launching a fleet of new state-run enterprises, the flagship of which was the new, expanded, state-owned electric utility, Hydro-Québec.

* * *

Some three millennia ago, humans discovered they could harness the power of rivers as well as that of animals, that wheels turned by falling water could drive flour mills, sawmills, forges, and other machines. Water wheels had to do their work beside rivers, for water power could not be transported. Then, little more than a century ago, came one of the most significant of the discoveries by which man now controls the forces of nature, and in doing so changes the world.

In October 1831, Michael Faraday, a blacksmith's son, a former bookbinder's apprentice and a scientist, discovered how to change the energy of motion into electricity. The principle Faraday discovered led to the dynamo. Before the end of his century, steam-powered dynamos were generating electricity for distribution and use within cities.

Though electric forces are manifest in nature, in forms such as lightning, the shock of an electric eel, and the mysterious lights known as Saint Elmo's fire, we do not harness energy from such sources. Like money, which is not a source but a medium for exchanges of wealth, electricity is not a source but a medium — an extraordinarily versatile one — for exchanges of energy. The energy in anything — in coal or oil; in uranium atoms; in wood, wind, sunshine or falling water — can be converted into electricity. In turn, electricity can be easily distributed, readily controlled, and cleanly converted into a host of services.

At first electricity made possible the telegraph and telephone, which in turn led to the radio, television and other techniques for communicating information. Then light bulbs, which convert electricity to clean, steady light, replaced smoking kerosene lamps in homes, and gas lamps on city streets. In vacuum cleaners, fans, washers, driers, and refrigerators, motors converting electricity to motion liberated women and servants from domestic drudgery. Electric railways moved people under and on city streets, and elevators lifted them within buildings that could now rise high above street level. Electricity made the climate indoors independent of that outdoors. Electric processing made aluminum, once rarer and costlier than gold, common and cheap. Power, once distributed only over short distances by clattering belts and pulleys, could now be distributed quietly, cleanly and widely through wires. The distinction between city and country began to disappear.

In this, the Age of Electricity, the relationship between science and technology changed. Before our time, practice preceded theory. The builders of the Gothic cathedrals knew nothing of the theory of the arch; the inventors of the steam engine knew nothing of thermodynamics. The genius of such men lay in their fingertips and in their experience. Thomas Edison, the inventor of the electric power system — of central generators feeding electricity through a web of wires to a multitude of light bulbs and other electricity converters — was the last of the empirical inventors. After Edison, science became the source not only of electrical but of all new technology, for the forces of nature manipulated in our time are so fundamental that they can no longer be grasped by practical intuition, but only by the abstractions of science.

Searching for a model of the phenomena with which he was experimenting, Faraday had formulated a vague notion of electromagnetic fields, regions of space through which invisible forces spread and interact. In 1864, James Clerk-Maxwell, a Scots physicist, published a set of elegant mathematical equations completely describing the behaviour of such electromagnetic fields. Faraday, like most of us, was mathematically naive. "There is one thing I would be glad to ask you," he wrote to

Maxwell. "When a mathematician engaged in investigation of physical actions and results has arrived at his conclusions, may they not be expressed in the common language as fully, clearly and definitely as in the mathematical formulae?"

But nothing in our experience equips us to grasp the whirling, waving complexity of force and energy in an electromagnetic field. What Maxwell's equations say so well cannot be said at all in ordinary language. Yet it is these equations that allow the forces of electricity and magnetism to be mastered, that led to the modern panoply of electrical technology. In the Age of Electricity, science, the restless search for new truth, became the source of technology, and the process of accelerating changes in technology began.

Like the railroad in the last century and the computer today, electric power was, for much of this century, the most glamorous technology, an emblem of progress, the way to a radiant future. "Communism," said Lenin, "is socialist power plus the electrification of the whole country."

Of all the natural sources of energy from which to generate electricity, the most attractive is falling water. One of the reasons for this is that water power is renewable. It is sunshine that drives the ceaseless cycle by which water evaporates, rises into and falls from the sky, and runs down to the sea. A river basin collects not only water, but also solar energy. Once built, a hydroelectric plant continues to produce power; it is a near approximation to a perpetual motion machine.[2]

A second reason for the attraction of hydroelectricity is that compared to other sources of electricity — to burning oil or coal, or splitting uranium nuclei — it appears much cleaner, for it produces no air pollution, no carbon dioxide, no nuclear wastes.

A third reason, I suspect, is that people are fascinated and frightened by great rapids and waterfalls, and awed by technology that masters such majestic forces. H. G. Wells, visiting the hall of dynamos at the Niagara Falls Power Company plant, the first major hydro plant in North America, reported being moved "to the depths of his soul by the vision of such vast power in the hands of man."[3]

Quebec's rivers, along which fur, timber and people were transported, had shaped its settlement and economy. Generating electricity represented a new way to convert this rich resource into wealth. Hydroelectric development began here early this century, and has continuously expanded. The first hydroelectric plants were built at those rare sites where large amounts of electric power could be generated, and where either there were nearby cities to which it could be shipped, or the power was so abundant and cheap that electricity-consuming industries could be enticed to build new plants near where it was generated.

English-speaking capitalists and engineers built the first major power-houses in this province, harnessing the Saint Lawrence River at rapids near Montreal, as well as tributaries of the Saint Lawrence where they tumbled off the central plateau of the Quebec-Labrador Peninsula. Montreal Light, Heat and Power Consolidated, for instance, supplied the large and growing market of Montreal with power generated nearby. It grew into one of the largest privately-owned electrical utilities in the world, and made Irish-born financier Henry Holt exceedingly wealthy. Shawinigan Water and Power Company, launched by American entrepreneurs, generated cheap and abundant electricity at Shawinigan Falls on the Saint Maurice River, a tributary of the Saint Lawrence. The company attracted aluminum refineries, pulp and paper mills, and other electricity-hungry industries to locate in what had been wilderness, and the surplus power flowed through North America's first long distance high-voltage transmission line to Montreal. On the Saguenay River, another tributary of the Saint Lawrence, a subsidiary of the Aluminum Company of America — a subsidiary which later became the multinational firm Alcan — built its own hydroelectric plants to power its aluminum refineries.

In the 1930s some French Canadians began criticizing these companies. In Ontario, other provinces of Canada, and many other jurisdictions around the world, electric utilities were publicly owned. In Quebec, the private companies were gouging their clients. And, most galling, they had English names, and their owners, the majority of whom were Americans, as well as their higher-echelon staff, all spoke English.

So the Quebec government began a two-stage nationalization — or rather, provincialization — of most of the private electric utilities. In April 1944 it bought, for a handsome sum, Montreal Light, Heat and Power Consolidated and its power-generating subsidiaries, and gave them to a new, publicly-owned electric utility known as Hydro-Québec. The young, French-speaking engineers and accountants who joined Hydro-Québec seized a golden chance to exercise their power and skill. With the Second World War over, business was picking up, and the demand for electricity was doubling steadily every ten years. To meet that demand, Hydro-Québec built ever-bigger hydro projects on rivers ever-farther from the centres of population and industry, running transmission lines at ever-higher voltages over ever-greater distances.

Then came the *Révolution tranquille*, and the second stage in the nationalization of the private electric utilities. The politician who orchestrated this second nationalization, René Lévesque, had been a popular television journalist. Every Sunday night during the late 1950s, he explained what was happening in the world to Quebecers. He was elected as a Liberal to the provincial parliament at the beginning of the Quiet Revolution, and became a cabinet minister, responsible for natural resources. He cleaned up the cosy system under which, in exchange for political contributions, engineers and contractors won contracts for building bridges, roads and power plants. Then he moved on "to decolonize the hydroelectric sector." In his memoirs, Lévesque recorded an interview with a "beefy red-head," a middle level executive who waved his whisky glass and asked "But Lévesque, how can people like you imagine you can run Shawinigan Water and Power?"[4]

"Of course," Lévesque recalled, "he was English-speaking and the company was English-owned, as they all were. I remember thinking, 'You bloody so-and-so. You're just like the British were a few years ago, saying the Egyptians could never run the Suez Canal.' It was the same paternalistic contempt — the colonial master speaking to the backward native. 'We'll show you, you bastard,' I thought. And we did."[5]

Campaigning under the slogan *"Maîtres chez nous"* (masters in our own house), Lévesque turned the 1962 provincial election into a virtual referendum on his proposal to nationalize the remaining private electric utilities in Quebec. He won. The newly-elected Liberal government respected the rules of capitalism in nationalizing the remaining private utilities. It bought them, virtually doubling Quebec's debt to raise the more than $600-million needed. And it did not touch companies, such as Alcan, which generated power from Quebec's rivers for their own use. "Six hundred million, and what for?" asked Pierre Trudeau, who later became Prime Minister of Canada. "To take over a business that already exists. It's just nationalistic suspender-snapping."[6] In Trudeau's view, all Lévesque's initiative would do is create jobs for the middle class at the expense of the working class; as indeed it did. The political goal of the Quiet Revolution was to replace an Anglo-American and Anglo-Canadian elite by a French one. Thus, after 1963, when Hydro-Québec doubled in size, it began to employ more people and spent more money every year than any other enterprise in Quebec, and more than most in Canada; and its language of work was French.

Hydro-Québec became a powerful lever for regulation of the provincial economy, one which the government used with the goal of getting jobs and power for Francophones. There were jobs with Hydro-Québec, and with the local suppliers which Hydro-Québec patronized through its policy of *achat chez nous* (buy at home). There was a tremendous increase in enrollment in engineering courses. Solid free enterprisers who had been muttering about socialism, came seeking contracts saying "Good, well now, we're good French-Canadians, so it's our turn. Before it was nothing but the Anglos."[7]

As well as serving the interests of French Canadian nationalists, there were other reasons driving Hydro-Québec's expansion. Since the beginning of this century until the 1970s, most utilities have been increasing the size of their power plants and the extent of their grid of power lines; this has enabled them to decrease production costs per unit of power, and thus maximize the return on the huge sums they invest in power plants, towers, transmission lines, lightning protection equipment, circuit breakers, transformers and all the other gear that constitute an electric power system.[8] Hydro-Québec, like other power utilities, felt this drive to expand. Unlike most other utilities, it had access to an extraordinary abundance of power in Quebec's wild, northern rivers. Harnessing these rivers would be technically challenging, for they ran through wilderness far from the cities. But now that the independent power plants and grids in Quebec had been integrated into Hydro-Québec, this utility had the financial muscle to undertake big, difficult projects.

At Expo '67, the World Fair held in Montreal in 1967, Québécois watched with pride a huge television screen showing the army of workers and fleets of trucks then building a dam — a giant, graceful structure of arched concrete — on the Manicouagan River, some 700 kilometres away. Technology usually advances in small steps, but to transmit power from the distant Manic hydroelectric complex, Hydro-Québec made a large extrapolation; it more than doubled the standard voltage used for high voltage long distance power transmission, and developed the first 735-kilovolt transmission line.

The next river to be plugged into the Hydro-Québec grid was even more distant from Montreal. The Churchill River flows east from the centre of the Quebec-Labrador peninsula into the Labrador Sea. At a site more than 1,000 kilometres from Montreal, it plunges down a rocky chute and out into space. This cataract was once one of the most awesome in the world. It could be heard from 15 kilometres away, and the Indians believed that the spirits who haunted it would strike dead those who gazed on it. When engineers came to gaze they saw a extraordinary concentration of water power.

Hydro-Québec did not develop Churchill Falls, which is in Labrador, the mainland portion of the province of Newfoundland and Labrador.[9] But Hydro-Québec was its only potential customer. After marathon negotiations, Hydro-Québec signed a deal with Brinco, the company developing the hydroelectric project. In return for securing the loans which paid for construction of the Churchill Falls hydroelectric plant, Hydro-Québec, for 65 years, gets almost all of its enormous output at what turns out to be extremely low prices — about one-fiftieth of those Hydro-Québec charges when it now sells power in the United States.

Hydro-Québec helped make Québécois masters in their own house not only by its economic functions of creating jobs and generating cheap electricity to fuel Quebec's economy, but also by its symbolic function of exciting national pride. Hydro-Québec partly substituted for the Church. Power has always been the chief manifestation of divinity. The engineers who turn the awesome power of waterfalls into electricity were seen as priest-like mediators between the ordinary and the Omnipotent; the transformation they effected was, like that the priests bring about at Mass, magical; and respect for Hydro-Québec's mastery and authority provided some of the social cohesion once provided by respect for the Church. And in building dams that — as the publicists put it — subjugated, vanquished, or conquered rivers, the utility showed the world that Québécois were as good as anyone else, including the English who had conquered, colonized, and humiliated them.

The engineers and administrators who ran this huge, complicated enterprise acquired sophisticated skills. Their example inspired confidence that Québécois could run modern businesses, or even a modern, independent state. Québécois were proud of *their* utility. "*Nous sommes tous Hydro-Québécois"* (we are all Hydro-Quebecers) they said. To question Hydro-Québec was unpatriotic. Immune from critical public scrutiny, more powerful in many ways than the government that was ostensibly in control — a relationship symbolized by the fact that the Montreal offices of the Premier of Quebec are within Hydro-Québec's headquarters — Hydro-Québec grew into a state within the state.

* * *

While the French were winning independence from the English, to the north of them the Indians and Inuit were engaged in a tougher struggle. Though industrial civilization had intruded on the southern fringes of the Quebec-Labrador Peninsula, forcing some Crees to make way for mining and forestry operations, most of the vast peninsula had no farm land or timber and, other than the great iron deposits straddling the Quebec-Labrador border, no known minerals. The land remained wild. Its people had modified many of their ways since first making contact with non-Natives. They played Scots fiddle tunes. Most believed in Christ, and read Bibles printed in a phonetic alphabet that Christian missionaries had invented for writing Cree. The missionaries set up rudimentary schools and nursing stations.

But despite the non-Native influences and services, they remained, basically, what they had always been: a hunting people. In the 1960s, the rhythm of the Crees' lives followed the seasons much as it had in the past — and much as it does to this day. Every spring, soon after the ice breaks, the geese fly north and the hunting season begins. (This period, when most Crees spend up to a month at hunting camps along the James Bay coast, is known as goose break.) They spent summers fishing, and socializing in their villages — which, in the 1960s, numbered seven, each a cluster of shacks without running water, a church, a Royal Canadian Mounted Police office, a Hudson Bay Company post, maybe a school. In the fall, some Crees traveled inland, by canoe or chartered plane, to spend winter in the bush. Each family group built a snug lodge, shot a supply of meat, and then trapped and hunted within a trapline, an area of several hundred square kilometres. They ate the meat of the fur-bearing animals they trapped, and small game and fish. At the end of March they harvested moose or caribou. In spring, they returned to the settlements, and the annual cycle started anew.

To subsist as hunters in a low-energy environment, the Crees scattered themselves in small groups across their land as sparsely as stars; in winter, their nearest neighbours would be, on average, more than 50 kilometres away. Though they fully occupied their land, to outsiders it seemed empty, a place of silence and great space.[10]

The hunting life can be hard. If the animals did not come — and populations fluctuate widely in northern ecosystems — a hunter and the people who depend on him to bring home food might starve. There are Crees now alive whose parents starved to death in bush camps. In 1922, Robert Flaherty's documentary film *Nanook of the North*, shot in northern Quebec, became a worldwide hit. A few years later its Inuit star starved to death.

Hunters could also freeze to death, or drown, or get shot by accident. Walter Hughboy, chief of the Cree village of Wemindji,[11] told me the story of his grandmother. She was shot in the arm while unloading a canoe, and gangrene set in. His grandfather heated his knife white hot and cut off her arm.

Or hunters could get sick. Non-natives brought many infectious diseases to which the Natives had no resistance. Smallpox, measles, influenza, scarlet fever, whooping cough, tuberculosis and other scourges have spread to the most remote Naskapi camp, and over the centuries, decimated the people of the sub-Arctic. Even in the 1960s, infant mortality among the Crees, as among all the Natives of Canada, was relatively high, and life expectancy relatively short.

But though the Crees and Inuit knew adversity, it would be false to picture their lives as a mere struggle for survival in a frigid and hence barely habitable land. Cold their land most certainly is, but in response to cold they are incredibly resourceful. Old men can still set off on long winter journeys, for example, equipped with little more than a kettle, an axe and a rifle. They welcome the cold, for it makes tracking, transport, and hunting easy. When a mild spell came in winter, and snowshoes and toboggans bogged down, then the Crees, by attaching a bundle of mistletoe to a dog's tail with a long string, setting the mistletoe on fire, and letting the dog run around on the ice, called the spirit of the north wind to bring back the cold.

Cold shapes their culture in many ways. "Beauty was judged on two things, chubbiness and a pretty face," a Cree writes in her autobiography. "Boys were not interested in a big bosom, a shapely figure, nice legs, or a well-rounded bottom. They did not get to see these things because the women and girls were always bundled from head to foot in layers of clothing."[12]

The essence of Cree culture has to do with hunting. To the Crees — to all hunting peoples — animals, trees, and the land itself are sacred, and killing animals is a religious occupation. When animals are willing to be killed they give themselves to hunters. Sometimes animal spirits appear to hunters in dreams, telling them where to hunt. Having received a gift, a hunter offers a gift in return. He puts a piece of meat into the fire so its smoke may carry thanks to the spirits. To show respect to the spirits and thus assure the success of future hunts, people should make full use of each animal, and observe rituals for disposing respectfully of its remains; they put the skull of a bear, a particularly honoured animal, in a tall tree with a view over a lake, for instance. Thus animals and man take care of each other, which is what they were put on Earth to do. And animals do take care of people; hunters in the sub-Arctic, though poor, live almost exclusively on the food that humans in virtually all cultures and at all times, most value: meat.

The Crees had no formal leaders. The people with authority were the elders, and those men who were responsible for traplines. Each trapline had a steward (now known as a tallyman) who looked after it. Stewards decided who could trap on a section of land, and when and where; they were effective wildlife managers, letting populations regenerate, avoiding harvesting more than the land could yield. They did not impose their decisions, but exercised their authority by suggestions and comments.

The stewards did not own the land. Owning, conquering, buying or selling land are concepts alien to Native traditions. The relation between humans and land, to them, is like that between children and a nourishing mother. They talk of Mother Earth; some of the Inuit of Northern Quebec call their country *amaamautilialuk* (she who is big and has breasts).[13]

Non-Natives stole the land, then encoded their claim in their law, the Native peoples now say. The European dispossession of the Natives of Canada was, as such things go, relatively benign. Europeans mainly settled the thin strip of land along the United States border. Canada is huge, and there were relatively few collisions between the new settlers and the original inhabitants. After the Confederation of Canada, the federal government pushed to sign formal treaties with the Indians, with whom they assumed the legal relationship of guardian to minor.

No treaties had been signed with the Crees or Inuit of the Quebec-Labrador Peninsula when, by 1912, the federal government had transferred title to the huge chunk of land they occupy — title whose legitimacy rests on that of the Hudson's Bay Company charter to Rupert's Land — to the province of Quebec. Though the terms of transfer by which Quebec obtained Nouveau-Québec — and thus doubled in size — obliged the province to make treaties with the Natives of New Quebec, it did not do so until 1975. To most French Canadians, except for a handful of lovers of austerity, ethnographers, botanists, and hunters, what lay between the Saint Lawrence Valley and the North Pole was a blank on the map, and the government of Quebec shrugged off any responsibility for its northern Natives.

In the 1960s, the federal government had taken over from fur traders and from missionaries as the dominant outside agent of change and the source of assistance in northern Quebec. It had made education compulsory for young Crees, who had to leave their villages and parents to spend the winter, the school year, in the South. One aim of this policy was assimilation. Though born in the bush, some of these children began to forget the languages, stories, and beliefs of their parents and grandparents. Federal agents organized a system of chiefs and band councils as a means of dealing with the Crees, of delivering rations and other services to them. The federal government also sent in Mounties to keep the peace and wave the flag. The people and institutions with which the Natives of New Quebec had contact — the fur traders, missionaries, policemen, Indian agents, and teachers — were English-speakers, and the Natives' second language was English.

In 1961, when the *Révolution tranquille* was gathering steam, René Lévesque tried, and failed, to order a cup of coffee in French in the Inuit village known then as Fort Chimo (now known as Kuujjuaq). He became the first Quebec politician to tour New Quebec. He pushed his government to claim its North by taking over from Ottawa. Quebec sent in French-speaking provincial police, and established French elementary schools.

Ancient ways and attitudes had survived in the Quebec-Labrador Peninsula as long as it was isolated, and its resources of no interest to industrial civilization. But among the French-speakers who came north in the 1960s, the first French-speakers that many Cree hunters ever met, were hydrological surveyors. They were gauging the power of the rivers emptying into James Bay, laying the foundations for future hydroelectric development.

NOTES

1. It is interesting to note that both the hunting society of the Quebec-Labrador Peninsula and that of Europe during the last ice age were fueled by caribou; though there are few caribou among the images on the cave walls at Lescaux, the painters littered the cave floors with caribou bones, cracked to get at the marrow. In Europe, caribou are now known as reindeer, so-called because the Laps of northern Europe have domesticated caribou and harnessed them to pull sleighs.

2. In practice, no hydroelectric power plant provides an endless flow of energy, for with time reservoirs fill with silt or dams spring leaks. In parts of the world where soil is thick, reservoirs silt up within decades. Siltation is not a significant problem in rocky northern Quebec; here dams are the limiting factor on the life of a hydro-electric project. For financial purposes, Hydro-Québec estimates the useful life of its dams at 50 years.

3. H.G. Wells, *The Future in America*, (Harper and Brothers, 1906), 54-55. Cited by David McCullough, *The Path Between the Seas; The Creation of the Panama Canal, 1870-1914*, (Simon and Schuster, 1977).

4. Lévesque, *Memoirs*, 181.

5. William Stockton, "René Lévesque and the Divided House of Canada," *New York Times Magazine* (20 May 1979).

6. Lévesque, *Memoirs*, 173.

7. See Jobin, *Les enjeux économiques de la nationalisation de l'électricité*. (My translation.)

8. For more on the interplay of technology and economics in the electric power industry see Hughes, *Networks of Power*.

9. According to Quebec, Labrador is no more than the narrow strip along the coast of the Labrador Sea where fishermen from Newfoundland have settled. According to Britain's highest legal authority, which settled the dispute in 1927, Labrador consists of all of the Quebec-Labrador Peninsula that drains into the Labrador Sea. Quebec maps either fail to show the border at all, or mark it as uncertain.

10. See Feit, "Hunting and the Quest for Power."

11. Wemindji was known as Paint Hills; hunters once ground rocks from the neighbouring hills into a red paint, which they put on the tips of their snowshoes to placate the spirits. In French, it is known as Nouveau-Comptoir.

12. Willis, *Geniesh*, 116.

13. Louis-Jacques Dorais, "L'avenir des minorités autochtones au Canada," *Bah'ai Studies Notebook* (Montreal, May 1986).

PART TWO
James Bay I

CHAPTER 2

Launching

Robert Bourassa, a lanky man with a slight stoop, prominent nose and horn-rimmed glasses, wanted to be Premier of Quebec ever since he was a teenager. After studying at Oxford and Harvard and becoming expert in public finance and taxation — subjects, he once acknowledged, that are "as boring as the rain"[1] — he was elected in 1966 to the parliament of Quebec as a Liberal. His speeches were often dull discourses on fiscal policy, but after marrying into a wealthy Quebec family, one with considerable industrial holdings, he had a well-stocked campaign fund and ready access to the captains of industry.

Bourassa moved, for a while, on the fringes of a circle of nationalists whose centre was René Lévesque. In 1968, Lévesque left the Liberals to found what became the Parti Québécois, a party whose first aim was to separate Quebec from the rest of Canada, to create a sovereign, independent nation.

"René," Bourassa said, "I can't join you. Political independence goes with monetary independence. Quebec cannot be sovereign and pay its bills with Canadian dollars."

"Monetary system, economic system," Lévesque replied, "all this is plumbing. One doesn't worry about plumbing when one fights for the destiny of a people."[2]

But Bourassa shrewdly chose plumbing — that is, regulating flows of water to generate electricity — as the central theme of his political career. In advocating unbridled hydroelectric development he could sound like a nationalist, for Hydro-Québec and its monumental dams had come to symbolize the emancipation of Québécois, but he did not have to make the politically risky commitment to independence.

Furthermore, in advocating hydroelectric development he sounded like a far-seeing economic leader. I once asked him about the origins of the James Bay project. The idea of building the James Bay project, he told me in his imperfect English, was the logical conclusion of a kind of economic theorem. "If we want to be a proud, strong people," he said, "it's not with independence we will achieve that goal, it's with economic strength. Where Quebec could increase its economic strength? It's with its natural resources, which are almost illimitable. Where we could have those natural resources? It was the North."[3] The resources he had in mind were the rivers.

In December 1969, when Bourassa was the opposition finance critic, he quizzed Hydro-Québec officials about Quebec's future energy needs. When, he wanted to know, were they were going to exploit the rivers flowing into James Bay?

As part of a systematic inventory of Quebec's power potential, Hydro-Québec had been studying these rivers sporadically since 1965, concentrating on the three big rivers in the southern part of the James

Bay region, the Nottaway, Broadback and Rupert. It was these rivers which Hydro-Québec would harness in its next hydroelectric project, but the utility had no intention of harnessing any rivers in the near future. Power galore was about to flow into its grid from Churchill Falls. Many of its engineers thought that Quebec's next power plant should be nuclear-powered. Nuclear power was a new, glamorous, sophisticated technology. It was going to provide abundant, cheap energy, many believed, and trigger a new industrial revolution. If Quebec kept building hydroelectric plants it would miss the wave of the future.

In the winter of 1969-1970, when Bourassa asked his questions of Hydro-Québec, he was campaigning for leadership of the Liberal party. Polls of voters indicated they wanted someone who would "bridge the gap between the generations" and be "strong enough to deal with Ottawa, the titans of finance, and most aspects of a highly sophisticated world." No one in the party came closer to this description than Robert Bourassa, who was then 36 years old. After a campaign in which hydroelectric development in the James Bay region was a main issue, Bourassa became Liberal leader in January 1970.

That April, after campaigning under the slogan *"Non au séparatisme"* (no to separatism), and after promising to create 100,000 jobs, he led his party to power. Three days after he became Premier, Bourassa told the president of Hydro-Québec to give priority to the James Bay dossier.

In his eagerness to dam the James Bay rivers, Bourassa had influential allies among whom François Rousseau was prominent. After retiring as Hydro-Québec's chief engineer, Rousseau had joined Acres (Québec) Limited, a consulting engineering firm.[4] Rousseau's job was to drum up fresh business for Acres, which would soon finish doing the engineering work on the Churchill Falls project. He spent many hours during the winter of 1968-1969 drawing dams on small-scale maps of the James Bay region — no detailed maps were then available — calculating and recalculating how many kilowatts the rivers could be made to yield, and at what price. He persuaded Paul Desrochers, Bourassa's principle adviser, that a James Bay hydroelectric project was technically feasible.

To find out if such a project was financially possible, if Hydro-Québec could borrow the money needed to build it, Bourassa flew to New York on Tuesday, October 6, 1970.

The day before, a small group of ultra-nationalists, members of the Front de libération du Québec, (the Quebec Liberation Front, or FLQ), had kidnapped James Cross, trade attaché at the British consulate in Montreal, and thus precipitated the October Crisis.

Acceding to one of the demands the kidnappers made for the release of James Cross, the French-language branch of the Canadian Broadcasting Corporation broadcast the FLQ manifesto. Within a year, the manifesto predicted — reworking Bourassa's campaign promise to create 100,000 jobs — a revolutionary army of 100,000 workers would take over Quebec.

Québécois did not answer the call to arms, but many cheered when they heard the manifesto read, for it aired grievances they had grumbled about, and injustices against which, in protest marches which often ended in battles with the police, they had demonstrated.

On Saturday, October 10, two men with drawn guns kidnapped Pierre Laporte, who was acting as Premier of Quebec while Bourassa was in New York. Bourassa returned that afternoon, and took refuge with his government in a Montreal hotel, sealed by police. Other than offering the kidnappers safe conduct to a foreign country if they released their hostages, he would not negotiate.

Days passed. Tension mounted. On Friday, October 16, Bourassa officially asked Pierre Trudeau, the Prime Minister of Canada, to invoke the War Measures Act, a law by which the federal government could assume sweeping and repressive power in order to put down insurrection. Before dawn, truckloads of soldiers and tanks were rolling into Montreal, and police were rounding up some 500 union leaders, artists, writers, and others suspected of nationalist sympathies.

How Pierre Laporte was strangled, James Cross freed, and the kidnappers caught and punished is not part of this story. What is relevant is that, by relying on Ottawa and the army to resolve the October Crisis, Bourassa looked to some like a wimp or, as Lévesque put it, like "a puppet of the federal rulers."[5] To redeem his image, Bourassa had to do something big and bold. He had to do something about his promise to create 100,000 jobs as well; the number of unemployed in Quebec, especially of unemployed young people, was large and growing.

* * *

On the evening of April 30, 1971, several thousand of the party faithful gathered in Quebec City's main hockey arena at a rally to celebrate the anniversary of the provincial Liberals' accession to power. It was before this partisan assembly that Bourassa launched the James Bay project.

First, the audience watched and listened to an audiovisual show — with music, narration, and images on three huge screens — vaguely but very enthusiastically describing roads pushing north into virgin territory, construction camps for tens of thousands of workers; the biggest hydroelectric plant ever to be built in Quebec; development of logging, mining, and commercial fishing; and billions of dollars of investment. "*Le monde commence aujourd'hui*" (the world begins today), declaimed a recorded voice as the show ended; and as the crowd chanted "Bou, Bou, Bourassa," the young Premier stepped on stage and savoured the tumultuous welcome for the project which he called — predictably — *le projet du siècle* (the project of the century).

Politically, the James Bay project was the Liberals' alternative to the Parti Québécois' independence project. The hydroelectric project would be, Bourassa said later, "the key to the political stability of Quebec."[6] Its political function was, in part, as a symbolic gesture stimulating hope and collective pride. Bourassa summoned Quebecers to meet "a fascinating challenge...the conquest of northern Quebec, its rushing, spectacular rivers, its lakes so immense they are veritable inland seas, its forests of coniferous trees...The whole history of Quebec must be rewritten. Our ancestors' courage and will must live again in the twentieth century. Quebec must occupy its territory; it must conquer James Bay. We have decided the time has come."[7]

Economically, a hydroelectric project could channel more money into Quebec than would a nuclear project. Most of the money would go to the Quebec-based suppliers of Hydro-Québec, especially to construction firms—construction is the largest single sector of the provincial economy—and to engineering firms. Neither construction nor engineering firms had had a major public works project to build since Expo '67.

Hydro-Québec, at first, was not sure the time had come. Building a massive hydroelectric project in the James Bay region was premature, some of the utility's staff felt, for the terrain had not been explored, and the power would not be needed in Quebec for some time. But Bourassa was Premier now. At a meeting with Hydro-Québec officials just before the project was launched, his political advisor Paul Desrochers yelled "The James Bay project is going ahead *with* or *without* Hydro-Québec."[8]

Bourassa attempted to bypass the utility. In July 1971 his government created a government-owned corporation, the Société de développement de la Baie James (the James Bay Development Corporation). Modeled on the Tennessee Valley Authority, its role was to oversee all development, including forestry, mining, and tourism, in the vast James Bay territory which, by government fiat, it now administered.[9] To oversee construction of hydroelectric projects in its territory, this corporation begat a subsidiary, the Société d'énergie de la Baie James (the James Bay Energy Corporation). The Energy Corporation was supposed to be another Hydro-Québec, more readily controlled by its political masters. Hydro-Québec, however, was not so easily circumvented. It took over the Energy

Corporation, and thus became master of the James Bay project which, it had now decided, should be built.

To make the kind of political impact he wanted to make, Bourassa needed a huge hydroelectric project. Independent of this motivation, both topography and what are called economies of scale dictated that any project generating hydroelectricity in the James Bay region for use elsewhere had to be huge. Nowhere in this region has nature concentrated water power as it has at Churchill Falls. To keep its production costs low Hydro-Québec itself would have to concentrate the water power by diverting water from several rivers into a central river. Before Hydro-Québec could build a dam in the wilderness it had to build infrastructure — roads and airports to get supplies and people in, camps to house them, power lines to get the power out — all at substantial cost. Once having paid a relatively fixed sum for infrastructure, then the more dams Hydro-Québec builds, the lower the cost per kilowatt generated tends to be. Thus economies of scale encourage building on a large scale. Bourassa and the managers of Hydro-Québec were planning to increase Quebec's power supply enormously without any clear idea as to where the power would be sold. Bourassa and his advisers had talked about the possibilities of exports to the United States with, among other influential people, bankers such as David Rockerfeller of the Chase Manhattan bank, his brother Nelson Rockerfeller, governor of New York, and presidents of utilities such as Consolidated Edison, which serves New York City. They had talked with French interests about the possibility of establishing an electricity-hungry uranium enrichment plant in Quebec. And they knew that domestic demand can be stimulated, and that the process of stimulating it begins with a demand forecast.

Since it takes ten years or more to build a big power plant, utilities must justify current decisions by peering into the future and estimating how much power their customers will need. Like other utilities, Hydro-Québec forecasts future demand by extrapolating from past trends. The consumption of electricity had been growing steadily since World War Two, doubling every ten years or so, as consumers bought refrigerators, air conditioners, electric hot water heaters and a host of other appliances, and as some factories switched to electric power. Hydro-Québec predicted that electricity demand in Quebec would continue to double every decade — or, more precisely, that it would grow at an average rate of 7.9 percent per year. The James Bay project had to be built, the utility said, to meet Quebec's growing appetite for electricity .

This sounded objective and precise, like the predictions scientists make about events at the ends of the universe or in the vortices of an atom. But forecasting the future demand for electricity is far from a precise science. At the time the James Bay project was launched, according to a Hydro-Québec planner, the utility arrived at its official forecasts through negotiation.[10] The engineers who planned and ran its power plants were optimistic in estimating future demand, for they were enthusiastic about building, and they feared running short of power. ("Quebecers," explained Robert Boyd, president and chief executive officer of Hydro-Québec, "would be the first to accuse us of incompetence and lack of foresight if we were unable to meet their electricity needs during the bitter cold of winter.")[11] The accountants who borrowed for the utility, on the other hand, were conservative in their demand estimates, for they feared that over-building could make further borrowing difficult. Negotiations between these two influential groups produced the utility's official forecast.

I suspect that Hydro-Québec's political masters had a voice in these negotiations too, for the demand forecast had to be high to justify building the huge James Bay project and it was higher than what other utilities with comparable markets were predicting.

One of the few people to question Hydro-Québec's forecasts at the time was Réal Boucher, then with Quebec's Ministry of Energy, and now a vice-president of Atomic Energy of Canada Limited. When, in the early

1970s, he suggested that there might be limits to the exponential growth in demand for electricity, the then president of Hydro-Québec told him, "Monsieur Boucher, you're questioning Hydro-Québec's growth rate. You are the enemy of Hydro-Québec."[12] Hydro-Québec saw its interests, now, as being allied with those of Bourassa. There were others, too, who stood to gain from the James Bay project.

* * *

In the summer of 1971 the estimated cost of the vaguely defined James Bay project was $6-billion, to be borrowed and spent over the coming decade. The ultimate source of many of the dollars that were borrowed for this project was the savings of elderly widows; women, because they generally live longer than men, collectively own a good deal of the savings of industrial societies. These savings are pooled and invested by insurance companies, pension funds and similar financial institutions.

One investment they can make is to loan money to a utility by buying a utility bond. A bond is a contract to pay interest regularly for a specified number of years — usually 30 in the case of Hydro-Québec's bonds — and, at the end of that period, to repay the sum of money borrowed.

The bond salesmen are investment bankers, money wholesalers, engineers of money flows. Hydro-Québec borrows so much that no one investment banking firm underwrites an entire issue of its bonds. Rather, a group of investment banking firms forms a syndicate to do so; that is, to purchase bonds, and to resell them to their clients. Until the 1960s, Quebec and Hydro-Québec borrowed from a Canadian syndicate dominated by the Bank of Montreal. This syndicate had close links with the private electric utilities in Quebec, and refused to finance their takeover. It was not difficult, however, for Hydro-Québec to borrow $300-million in New York, and since then Hydro-Québec has done the bulk of its borrowing on Wall Street.

The man responsible for borrowing the money needed to pay for the James Bay project was Hydro-Québec's treasurer, Georges Lafond. He joined Hydro-Québec in 1965, soon after the second nationalization. Lafond recalls that his friends at Standard and Poor's and at Moody's — firms which rate the credit worthiness of institutions that borrow by issuing bonds — said that it would not be possible for Hydro-Québec to finance the James Bay project alone; it would need provincial and federal government money. But Lafond, who has the skills both of a diplomat and of a salesman, persuaded the investment bankers and the institutional investors to have confidence in Hydro-Québec.

One of Lafond's arguments was that putting money into dams and powerhouses and transmission lines is an inflation-free investment. Hydro-Québec would have to spend something on maintenance, of course, but would not have to buy fuel, whose cost can rise with inflation. A hydroelectricity plant, once built, will produce electricity, and hence revenue, as long as the water runs. He also pointed out that loans to Hydro-Québec for the James Bay project were guaranteed by the government of Quebec, and further secured by the fact that Hydro-Québec, through its subsidiary, the Energy Corporation, controlled the project, and had awarded the contract to manage it to an American engineering firm renowned for managing megaprojects.

Hydro-Québec's engineers only do preliminary studies of its projects. Consulting firms do the detailed engineering. Hydro-Québec buys more engineering services than any other Canadian electric utility. Its policy is to develop Quebec consultants' savoir-faire — and, some say, to prevent Hydro-Québec's unionized engineering staff from acquiring power. The biggest of the home-grown consulting engineering firms was Surveyer, Nenniger et Chénevert (SNC), which had worked on the Manic project.

Building the James Bay project was not going to present engineering challenges like those the Manic project did, with its ambitious, concrete dam. The technical problems of designing the elements of the James Bay hydroelectric project were going to be routine, for its elements, massive piles of rock and earth, were little more sophisticated, as structures, than the Pyramids. But the James Bay project was going to be an extravaganza of earth-moving. (The builders of the first phase of the La Grande complex have, at sites scattered over a vast wilderness, moved more than enough earth to pile up 80 replicas of the Great Pyramid of Cheops.) The real challenge was going to be that of orchestrating the work of many people and the flow of many materials, of attending to a dazzling complexity of details so that things meshed, so that jobs got done properly, on time and on budget, and to do all this far from industrial civilization. Hydro-Québec was going to design and manage the construction of the James Bay project transmission lines, but neither the utility, nor the Energy Corporation, was going to manage the construction of the hydroelectric megaproject. That job would be done, on a lucrative contract, by an engineering firm, or firms.

Bourassa's advisers had been meeting with representatives of the San Francisco-based firm Bechtel International, one of the largest engineering and construction firms in the world. It has built refineries, chemical plants, pipelines, oil wells, and cities, around the world. Its subsidiary, Canadian Bechtel, managed the construction of the Iron Ore Company's mining operations and the Churchill Falls hydroelectric project, both in Labrador.[13] Bechtel has developed a system for managing megaprojects; it specializes in organizing specialists, of whom it has an enormous pool to draw from, including many who speak French, the language in which the James Bay project would be built.

Consulting engineering firms are, like libraries, common pools of knowhow and talent, and Bechtel had one of the broadest and deepest pools in the world. But the choice of the firm to which the contract to manage the James Bay megaproject would be awarded was not just a choice of the most competent, for building megaprojects is not just an exercise in solving technical problems. It requires access to powerful politicians and financiers, a service which big consulting firms, such as Bechtel, also provide.

In September 1972, Robert Boyd, president of the James Bay Energy Corporation, announced the award of the contract to manage the James Bay project to Bechtel Québec, which would work in partnership with a Quebec firm, Lalonde, Valois, Lamarre, Valois et Associés (LVLVA).

Bernard Lamarre, a jovial, flamboyant, corpulent, hustling, workaholic engineer, had married the daughter of one of the founders of a small engineering firm, and became one of its owners. LVLVA prospered during the years of the Quiet Revolution, building for the government the public works by means of which Quebec was modernizing: roads, schools, bridges, tunnels, and the Expo 67 site. In the early 1970s, the firm had several hundred employees, but the building boom was ending. Lamarre had been hunting for work for his firm, and had outfoxed SNC which, in consortium with two other Quebec-based firms, had been lobbying for the contract to manage the James Bay project. The management contracts were for a fixed percentage on top of costs. Bechtel, it was later revealed, got $36-million and LVLVA $19-million.[14] With this its first big contract, the upstart Quebec engineering firm sprouted into the corporate empire known as Groupe Lavalin or, simply, Lavalin.

The Parti Québécois, the opposition party, led a storm of protest against the James Bay project. According to Jacques Parizeau, the party's economic adviser (and now its leader), the hydroelectric project was "sheer delirium." Hydro-Québec should be building nuclear plants. "Just because a river is French-Canadian and Catholic," he said, "it's not absolutely necessary to put a dam on it."[15] The selection of Lamarre's firm, René Lévesque suspected, was "a consolation prize for the voracious entourage of the Bourassa government."[16] The project, critics suggested, was simply a vehicle for political patronage on a lavish scale.

NOTES

1. L. Ian MacDonald, *From Bourassa to Bourassa: A Pivotal Decade in Canadian History* (Harvest House, 1984), 297.
2. Jean Pelletier, "The Resurrection of Bourassa," *Saturday Night* (February 1984): 13.
3. Robert Bourassa, interview with author, Montreal, 13 April 1985.
4. In 1970, after Rousseau became a partner in Acres (Québec), and in response to anti-Anglo sentiment, the firm was renamed Rousseau, Sauvé, Warren.
5. Lévesque, *Memoirs*, 249.
6. Lacasse, *Baie James*, 120. (My translation.)
7. Bourassa, *James Bay*, 10.
8. Lacasse, *Baie James*, 114. (My translation.)
9. The James Bay territory consists of the drainage basins of the Nottaway, Broadback, Rupert, Eastmain, and La Grande Rivers (all of which flow into James Bay); of the Great Whale River (which flows into Hudson Bay); and a portion of the basin of the Caniapiscau River (which flows into Ungava Bay). Its total area, 350,000 square kilometres, is one-fifth that of Quebec.
10. Hafsi, *Le changement radical*, 131.
11. Robert Boyd, "D'un projet contesté à une réalisation incontestable," *Forces* 48 (1979): 4-17.
12. Réal Boucher, interview with author, Montreal, 10 December 1985.
13. Acres had been responsible for the Churchill Falls design and engineering.
14. Roger Lacasse, "L'adversité: un élément de cohésion et de réussite," *En Grande* (May 1983): 8.
15. Lacasse, *Baie James*, 129.
16. Lacasse, *Baie James*, 228.

CHAPTER 3

Resisting and Compromising

Neither Bourassa nor his government had consulted any of the approximately 5,000 Crees and 3,500 Inuit living in northern Quebec in the early 1970s about the James Bay project before launching it, or even informed them. "We must conquer the North," Bourassa had written, and conquerors are not courteous.

The Natives learned about the project from news reports of its launching. Philip Awashish, for instance, read in a day-old *Montreal Star* that, among other things, the Rupert River was to be dammed. This, he suspected, meant that the land where his family hunted, fished and trapped would be flooded.

Awashish was one of the first generation of Crees to have completed secondary school. He, and a number of other young Cree men whom he had met while away from home at school, straddled two cultures, that of the bush and that of the city. They felt that they should and could resist the government's hydroelectric project.

Many Crees laughed and shook their heads in disbelief when young men like Awashish told them that their land might be flooded to generate electricity. They had no clear concept of the technology that was about to intrude on their lives. Electricity was new to the Crees; they had only recently coined a word for it in their language: *nimischiiuskutaau* (fires of thunder). To light such a fire, they were told, rivers were going to be made to run backward into huge artificial lakes, and then the fire — or, as some understood it, the water — was going to run south through power lines. It sounded like an insane and terrible scheme.

Awashish helped organize a meeting at the end of June 1971 in Mistissini,[1] his home, at which representatives from all of the eight Cree villages in northern Quebec gathered together for the first time ever. This began the process by which the Crees of Quebec have come to see themselves as belonging not just to family and village, but to a regional ethnic and political unit, to a nation. Having, at that time, no regional political organization, the Crees began organizing under the auspices of the Indians of Quebec Association, one of a number of groups which the federal government had begun financing so that aboriginal peoples could be represented in negotiations on land claims. This association mainly represented Indians of southern Quebec.

Lawyers working for the Indians of Quebec Association explained to the Crees gathered in Mistissini that Quebec considered itself sole owner of all the lands the Crees used. At the end of their meeting, the Crees drafted a resolution: "We, the representatives of the Cree bands that will be affected by the James Bay hydro project or any other project, oppose to these projects [sic] because we believe that only the beavers had the right to build dams in our territory..." They asked Jean Chrétien, then the federal Minister of Indian Affairs and Northern Development, and thus their legal guardian, "to stop any attempt of intrusion of [their] rightful owned territory by…Quebec…"

Though Chrétien felt sympathy for the Crees, he would not put any pressure on Quebec, for his government did not want to thwart Bourassa, its chief bulwark against separatism. Furthermore, Ottawa wanted to shift responsibility for Indians to the provinces. The federal government, therefore, assumed an attitude of "informed neutrality." It did, however, give the Indians of Quebec Association some half-million dollars to help pay for fighting the James Bay project. With that money, early in 1972, the Indians of Quebec Association hired Philip Awashish and Billy Diamond — the 21-year-old chief of Waskaganish,[2] the village at the mouth of the Rupert River — to begin organizing the Cree resistance to the James Bay project.

They were helped and guided by a handful of sympathetic non-Natives with useful skills and connections, such as Harvey Feit, an anthropologist. In the early 1970s, Feit was doing doctoral research on the hunters of the Cree community of Waswanipi. He persuaded his research director, Richard Salisbury of McGill University in Montreal, to help raise funds for the meeting of Crees at Mistissini, and to write to Bourassa, protesting the absence of either environmental or social impact studies of the proposed hydroelectric project. The Crees were also advised by James O'Reilly, a lawyer. He used to play hockey with some Mohawk Indians from southern Quebec, and this friendly connection led to the Indians of Quebec Association hiring the law firm for which he then worked.

The coterie of non-Native advisers to the Cree grew as the core people recruited others, mainly in English-speaking circles, and particularly at McGill. When, for instance, Feit learned that John Spence, a biologist newly-arrived at the university, had done research on the impacts of dams on fishes, Feit and Awashish visited him. Indians, it turned out, had fascinated John Spence ever since, as a boy growing up in Northern Ireland, he had heard and read about Methodist missions to

North American Natives. He was eager to do something practical, such as studying the ecological impacts of the James Bay project, and he relished the prospect of a fight.

This was the beginning of the 1970s, and environmental consciousness was seeping into Canada. Governments established the first environmental ministries, academics founded the first environmental journals, and citizens became active in environmental issues. The James Bay project was the first big issue for the nascent environmental movement in Quebec. Many of the citizens who supported the Crees and opposed the hydroelectric project had connections with McGill University. One of the persons organizing grassroots opposition was Hélène Lajambe, then an economics student at McGill. In 1970, she helped found La société pour vaincre la pollution (SVP, or Society to Overcome Pollution), the first French-speaking ecological group in North America. When she first heard about the James Bay project, she thought it was so stupendously big it would never get off the ground, but as it picked up steam, so did she.

She opposed the project for a number of reasons. She is a militant environmentalist, and it is almost a tenet of environmentalism that dams despoil. As well, she objected to what seemed to her, and others, to be the callous contempt of the developers for the Indians. She told me that she attended a meeting once in Bourassa's office at which Robert Boyd, head of the James Bay Energy Corporation, said of the Crees: "I know them well. I've been up there three or four times. They're all lazy."[3] In October 1971, Lajambe and others organized a meeting on the James Bay project at which they screened the audiovisual show with which Bourassa had launched the project that spring. The Crees at the meeting laughed on seeing images of bison supposedly grazing on the James Bay coastal plain. The joke escaped Hélène, until it was explained to her that there are no bison in the sub-Arctic. She had never been to James Bay, and had no idea what kind of place it was. Few people had. Only a handful of life-scientists had ever visited the region, and few of their studies were recent.

John Spence and his wife Gillian prepared a report on the ecological implications of the James Bay project, which they presented at a workshop at McGill in January 1972, organized by Lajambe and others. No one had ever studied the impacts of creating reservoirs in northern Canada, and the James Bay reservoirs were going to be farther north than any others. Apart from sparse literature on the effects of dams elsewhere — most of which described southern, not northern conditions — all the Spences had to go on was theory. The gist of their report was a diagram of the James Bay ecosystem. At the top were the Crees. Below, linked by arrows symbolizing the links of the food chain, were the animals on which the Crees depended for food. Because the hydroelectric project could disturb many of these links, making it harder for the Crees to harvest food, the Spences recommended the hydroelectric scheme be reconsidered.

A few weeks later, in February 1972, a group composed mainly of government employees issued another preliminary report on the impacts of the James Bay project, after some months of researching the sparse literature. "It was a bust," said Richard Salisbury of McGill, a member of this Federal-Provincial Task Force on the Environment. "People didn't know much about northern ecology, certainly not compared to the Native people. Most of the stuff on dams and water was derived from experience on the Aswan Dam, in Egypt. There was almost nothing in the scientific literature about northern lakes, except for Lake Baikal."[4]

In the preamble to its report the task force stated that it assumed that questions about the need for the electricity "had been adequately considered by the authorities prior to making their decision to proceed." It recommended turning the James Bay region into a "large-scale natural laboratory" for studying the impact of major developments in the North and suggested that the altered ecosystem "may be just as satisfactory as the original natural system." The only potentially alarming impact of the project, according to its report, would be on the Natives. And it recommended building first on the La Grande River, where a hydroelectric project would have less impact on nature and people than one farther south, on the Nottaway, Broadback, and Rupert Rivers.

* * *

Early in 1972, Billy Diamond and Philip Awashish were touring the Cree villages, informing people about the hydroelectric project and helping hammer out a consensus on how to respond. Diamond, a big man with lots of chutzpah, was honing his aggressive political style. At a meeting in his home village, Waskaganish, he denounced the Federal-Provincial Task Force report for saying that Indians had become strongly dependent on the white man's society, and because the report's summary — which omitted this and other claims — had been poorly translated into Cree. Stirred up, the audience burned their copies of the report in the wood stove that heated the community hall.

Boyce Richardson, then a journalist with the *Montreal Star*, was there, and described the scene in his book *Strangers Devour the Land*. He would have liked, he wrote, "to be able to report that the angered crowd, stirred to great passion by their intense desire to defend their culture, rioted and burned down the cinema." But he was disappointed; the Crees were having fun, and stayed around to watch a movie called *Nashville Revels.*[5]

The consensus emerging among the Crees was that they could not stop the hydroelectric project, but they should try to negotiate modifications to it in order to protect their hunting, trapping, and fishing economy. They had always willingly adopted whatever modern devices made their lives easier and safer. They did not view the traditional way of life through the romantic haze which clouds many urban dwellers' view of Natives. They were willing to change, but they wanted some control over that change, over what would happen in their lands.

Neither Bourassa, the provincial government, nor its agencies, the James Bay Development Corporation and the Energy Corporation, would consider any modifications to the hydroelectric project. They would do no more than inform the Crees as the plans evolved — as they did, in May 1972, when the engineers decided to begin the James Bay project with a complex centred on the La Grande River. The project was going ahead no matter what the Indians wanted. James O'Reilly, who had left the firm for which he had been working when it accepted the James Bay Development Corporation as a client, and set up his own law firm specializing in Native law, advised the Crees to fight the project in court. In April 1972, they asked the Superior Court of Quebec to order a halt to all work on the James Bay project because it was irrevocably and adversely affecting them. They also asked John Spence to organize a field trip to gather the ecological data they would need to support this argument in court.

"The Crees sometimes get real turkeys as consultants," Spence told me. "Basically they hire people they feel comfortable drinking with, and all kinds of social outcasts have been pissing away Cree money. Chrétien expected the $100,000 [for the field trip] would be pissed away. But O'Reilly was decent. He gave me a cheque, and said get the best team you can together."[6]

Spence assembled some 15 wildlife experts. In August 1972 they flew north, to Fort George, the Cree community at the mouth of the La Grande River, and from there they scattered throughout the James Bay territory. With two guides, Stephen Tapiatic and his son Eddy, and a pilot, Spence flew in a Beaver aircraft up the length of the La Grande from its mouth. They stopped first about 37 kilometres upstream from James Bay at the rapids where the engineers planned to build the La Grande-1 dam and powerhouse. The whitefish were making their annual run up from the sea to spawn, and people from Fort George were deftly netting them.

There was tea brewing on twig fires. Spence amused the kids with instant Polaroid pictures, and collected the egg-crammed ovaries of female whitefish, proof that the rapids were a spawning ground.

Spence and his party flew upstream, past rapids over which helicopters were zooming and where the La Grande powerhouses now stand. His guides won Spence's respect for their intimate knowledge of the vast land and its life forms. It was a nomad's knowledge. Stephen Tapiatic had crossed the Quebec-Labrador Peninsula three times. He would leave Fort George at the beginning of winter, paddle up the La Grande until freeze-up, then continue on snowshoes over the height of land and down the Caniapiscau River, arriving at Ungava Bay with the summer.

Through their much more modest journeys, Spence and his fellow scientists began to know the James Bay ecosystem. "When we came back we could say we had been there," Spence told me. "We were experts." To build the James Bay project, he now declared, would be to commit cultural genocide. His colleagues at McGill told him that he was no longer doing science but politics. "You're right," he replied. "But it's a political project, so let's have a political solution."

* * *

Flying back to Montreal from Fort George, in August 1972, Gillian Spence overheard construction workers who were returning from La Grande-2. The Crees lived in squalor, the workers said, and were of sub-normal intelligence. The Indian women could be bought for the price of a drink, and the men could not be trusted; they would drop their tools and go hunting if a flock of geese flew overhead. The James Bay territory belonged to Quebec, and now that the Québécois were developing it, the Crees would have to adapt. The developers, too, were disdainful of the Indians, and justified as inevitable the disruption the hydroelectric project would cause. Their position, basically, was that the Natives were squatters on the land, who might have privileges to harvest wildlife, but never having done anything to develop its other resources, had no rights to them. In October 1972, representatives of both the Crees and the Inuit of Northern Quebec met with Bourassa and his ministers in his Quebec City offices. Malcolm Diamond, Billy's father, began a ceremonial speech in Cree about his love of the land. Bourassa showed his impatience and left the meeting, gravely offending the Natives. And, in a speech that autumn, Gilles Massé, Quebec's Minister of Natural Resources, said that "the radical transformation of [the Crees'] lifestyle, which is the basis of their culture, is inevitable...it will have to take place in a few decades at the most."[7]

The Natives fought back. In November 1972, acting for both the Crees and Inuit of Northern Quebec, James O'Reilly asked the Superior Court of Quebec to ban construction work at James Bay until the judicial system had decided whether to grant the permanent injunction he had already requested. Usually, judges settle such temporary injunction actions quickly, but the hearings that then began before Judge Albert Malouf were unusually complex and long.

After first convincing Malouf that the Natives appeared to have rights in the James Bay territory, O'Reilly then began putting more than 60 of them on the stand in Montreal. Carefully coached by O'Reilly, speaking for the most part through translators, they explained themselves to the urban world which many of them had never before visited. They talked about fishing, hunting and trapping, about their reverence for the land, about their reliance on it for what they call country food: for bear, beaver, caribou, moose, rabbit, seal, and whale; for geese and ptarmigan; for Arctic char, pike, salmon, sturgeon, trout, walleye, and whitefish.

O'Reilly then called on expert witnesses to describe the hydroelectric project and to predict its impacts on the ecosystem. One of these witnesses was Einar Skinnarland, an engineer who, after working on many hydroelectric projects, including Churchill Falls, had "second thoughts about aspects of them, especially [about] wholesale river diversions, the most disastrous of the decisions we make," and who believed that the James Bay project was "too big" and that the forecasts of electricity consumption justifying its size were "baloney."[8] Skinnarland explained to Malouf how the James Bay project was being built, how rivers would be dammed, diverted, and flooded so as to form huge reservoirs, how the water level in these reservoirs would fluctuate widely and unnaturally. Arguing on the basis of what they had learned on their ecological field trip to the James Bay region that August, Spence and the other wildlife specialists predicted, among many other things, that the flooding and the fluctuating reservoirs would destroy such habitats as spawning grounds, nesting sites, and the shorelines on which beaver depend. The defendants in the action — Hydro-Québec, the James Bay Development Corporation, and the James Bay Energy Corporation — began to state their case in March 1973. The mastermind of their defense was Armand Couture, a co-owner, with Bernard Lamarre, of the engineering firm Lavalin, and a member of the five-man committee managing the James Bay project. The developers, he told me, felt alone. They could not find a scientist in Canada to testify on their behalf and were astounded by the "emotional fervour" of the opponents of the project. Couture prides himself on having created "an atmosphere of honest rivalry" in the courtroom. "We acted like gentlemen," he told me. "Every morning in court we shook hands with the representative for the Indians and wished them *'Bonne chance'*. Because we met like that every day, for several weeks, there even developed a certain friendship between us. It is the principal characteristic that enabled us later to negotiate with them and to reach agreement."[9]

The developers' case boiled down to three arguments. First, country food accounted not for more than half the Native diet, as the Indians argued, but for less than a quarter. They no longer lived primarily off the land, in other words, but off the government: they bought most of their food, and the other things they used, with the money they received in the form of family allowances, old age pensions, and the like. They had no right to oppose development on the grounds that it would harm their traditional life because they had abandoned that life.

Second, the environmental impacts of the hydroelectric project would be mild. Flooding the reservoirs, for instance, would only increase the seven percent of the James Bay territory naturally under water by a further three percent, and the impacts of this would be mitigated.

Third, halting construction would inconvenience all the people of Quebec, who would need more electricity; since there were far more Quebecers than Natives, the interests of the majority should prevail over those of the minority.

After 71 days in the courtroom, after hearing more than 150 witnesses, Judge Albert Malouf spent the summer of 1973 preparing his decision. While he did so, the struggle over the James Bay project, a struggle for which his courtroom served as the first battlefield, continued. Or rather, the struggles continued — for the James Bay project serves as a focus for three distinct power struggles: between aboriginal hunters and industrial society, between environmentalists and industrial developers, and the endless Canadian squabble between French and English.

* * *

In February 1972, Hélène Lajambe and others had formed Le comité pour la défense de la Baie James, known in English as the James Bay Committee, to organize environmental opposition to the hydroelectric project among Quebecers. Lajambe and her colleagues worked to build a coalition: it included hunting and fishing groups in Quebec; environmental, nature and conservation organizations in Quebec and Canada; the two major Quebec Native peoples' groups, the Indians of Quebec Association and the Quebec Métis and non-Status Indians Association; anti-poverty groups; the Atlantic chapter of the Sierra Club; and more.

Tirelessly, she and others argued against the project.[10] They predicted environmental catastrophes. The weight of the water to be accumulated in the reservoirs of the James Bay project could trigger earthquakes. By delaying the natural flood of melt water in the spring, the dams would delay the break-up of sea ice in Hudson Bay, chill the Labrador current which sweeps down the east coast of the continent, and thus prolong winter throughout the Northeast; the effects would be felt as far south as New York City. One environmental activist told me that to this possibility Bourassa replied "Well, we'll just have to wear extra sweaters."[11]

They also made economic arguments. The hydroelectric project would create relatively few temporary jobs, and the cost per job created would be exorbitant. By increasing inflation and public debt, it would make Quebec's economic problems worse. Why not reduce demand for electricity rather than increase its supply? Why not build nuclear power plants? (In the early 1970s, many environmentalists approved of nuclear power.) The environmentalists campaigned for a halt to the hydroelectric project until its impacts had been studied, until the public had been consulted, and until the Native peoples had freely consented to it.

In April 1973, while the Malouf hearings were still under way, the James Bay Committee held public hearings in Montreal into the hydroelectric project — something which Bourassa had refused to do, and still refuses to do. As a gesture of support for the Native peoples, and to raise money for the struggle, they put on a show hosted by Gilles Vigneault, the beloved Québécois singer and songwriter, the composer of Quebec's unofficial *hymne national* (national anthem). "One could build a stairway with tombstones from the cemetery of Indian culture," he said, "but I would never climb this stairway, even if it led to Quebec's independence."

Then, as now, coverage of the James Bay project in news media both inside and outside Quebec tended to criticize Quebec. The developers were accustomed to adulation as national heroes. According to Laurent Hamel, chief of the La Grande-2 construction camp and a man who had spent his life building dams for Hydro-Québec, they felt they were being maligned by "a systematic campaign of denigration." "I was almost ashamed to say that I was working at Baie James," he reported. "I had the feeling I was working against my country."[12]

But, in fact, relatively few Québécois were opposed to the hydroelectric project. Quebec's economy was based on chopping down trees, digging up rocks, and damming rivers. Its territory was so immense and so rich in natural resources that most felt that *quand il n'y en aura plus, il y en aura encore* (when we run out, there's always more). Wilderness was a hostile force, not to be conserved tenderly but mastered forcefully. Master it the Québécois did, at brutal cost to the environment. Montreal and other major cities poured raw sewage, and other filth, into Quebec's rivers. Toxic fumes from smelters and mines wasted its forests. Quebec was, and in many respects remains, *le paradis de la pollution*.[13]

Canadians are less likely than Americans to question authority, and tend to rely more on government to run things. The tradition of public scrutiny of authority is particularly shallow in Quebec, and the aboriginals of the James Bay region are by no means unique in having the government impose a megaproject on them without consultation.

Some Québécois dismissed the grassroots opponents of the James Bay Committee as members of the counterculture, *les granolas*, as silly idealists. Others suspected scheming Anglos of fomenting opposition to the James Bay project in order to thwart Québécois in their efforts to master their own destiny. Many of the groups supporting the James Bay Committee, after all, had English names, and the Crees and Inuit of Quebec all preferred English to French as their second language.

In October 1973, fed up with the hassles of the court case, John Spence returned to the James Bay country to fish and to gather data on fish. With Stephen Tapiatic, he paddled down the La Grande River. The geese were flying south, the weather was fine, and the country was beautiful, seemingly unspoiled. Then they began to hear a continuous rumbling. It was the noise of earth being moved at the La Grande-2 construction site.

Some of that noise stopped, briefly, the following month. In November 1973, after deliberating for almost five months, Judge Albert Malouf made his ruling. James O'Reilly, whom the Crees call *Mashimanitou* (the sorcerer), had earned his nickname: the judgement was a strong one. In essence, Malouf held that the developers were trespassing in the James Bay region and, since their works "will have devastating and far-reaching effects on the Cree Indians and the Inuit," he ordered the developers to stop until the Natives' case for a permanent injunction had been heard.[14]

Within a week, the Quebec Appeals Court suspended Malouf's ban because, the court reasoned, the people of Quebec, in whose interest the project was being built, were more numerous than the Natives, who wanted it stopped.

Both the hydroelectric project, and the court actions to stop it, went ahead, but Malouf's decision had strengthened the Natives' position and weakened Quebec's. Though it had undertaken to do so, Quebec had not settled the land claims of its northern Natives. They could sue again, and the courts might rule that they had rights to the land, rights which Malouf's ruling had recognized at least morally, if not legally.

Fearing a legal impasse, which in turn might give the investors in the hydroelectric project cold feet, Bourassa had to settle with the Natives. He offered a treaty, the terms of which included, among other things, payment of $100-million. In March 1974, Cree hunting families were flown out of bush camps to vote on this offer. They rejected it. "The Indian lands are not for sale, not for millions and millions of dollars," said Billy Diamond. In fact, he and the other Cree leaders and their advisers were calculating that, though they could not stop the hydroelectric project, they could hold out for better terms; and so, early in 1974, as work on the hydroelectric project proceeded, intense negotiations began.

The negotiations were not about deciding who is landlord and who is tenant in northern Quebec, though that thorny question was — and remains — at the heart of the dispute over the James Bay project. As I understand it, the essence of most Natives' position on this question is that the land which the Creator gave to them was stolen by newcomers, whose governments then legalized the theft. To win the control over their own affairs that they want, the Natives have to translate their claims from their own cultural terms into those of the newcomers. And so they argue within the non-Native legal system — a system, they say, set up by and for a society of thieves — that they were landlords when the newcomers arrived, and remain so. They have no title to the land, but an aboriginal right to it; they were occupying, using, and controlling it when Europeans arrived; they were there first.

The essence of the government's position is that to redeem long past injustices is impossible; that the Natives benefit enormously from the technology, enterprise, and wealth of the non-Native development of the country; and that the concept of aboriginal rights is too vague to be workable.

The premises and claims of the contending parties are incompatible. The Natives are not going to give up their ethnic distinctiveness and assimilate. The non-Natives are not going to give up the country they have built. To resolve this impasse, the dominant power, the federal government, proposes that Native peoples, after negotiation, accept limited and clearly-defined forms of self-government under provincial jurisdiction and, in exchange, give up their claim to aboriginal rights. Ottawa has been funding Native groups since the beginning of the 1970s to enable them to research and present their claims under this process, and it treated the negotiations with the Natives of northern Quebec as the first comprehensive land claim under its new process.

With funding from the federal government, then, the Crees set up their first political organization, the Grand Council of the Crees (of Québec). Billy Diamond became Grand Chief, as well as chief of the Cree negotiating team. The Inuit counterparts were the Northern Quebec Inuit Association, and its founder and head, Charlie Watts. They were negotiating with representatives of the governments of Canada and of Quebec, and of the developers, Hydro-Québec, the James Bay Development Corporation, and the James Bay Energy Corporation. Each side had its battery of lawyers and expert advisers.

Time was on the developers' side.[15] As work on what was being billed as the greatest construction project in the world advanced, as more billions of dollars poured into it, the chances of stopping it receded, and so too did the threat the Natives posed to it. The Natives believed that the hydroelectric project could probably not be stopped, that they were inevitably going to lose some of their traditional land, and that it would be better to lose with a treaty than without one. This, in turn, meant that they were resigned to the surrender of their aboriginal rights.

What the negotiations were about, mainly, was the definition of the specific rights for which the Natives would surrender their aboriginal rights. The Crees wanted, above all, to preserve their traditional life style. "We are the hunting people," is the meaning of their self-definition in their own language; and so they were bargaining for land to be set aside on which only Crees could hunt, trap, and fish. As well, they wanted as much autonomy as they could get. For instance, they wanted to take over the administration of the hospitals, schools, and other institutions serving their communities from distant, paternalistic, non-Native bureaucrats. They wanted procedures to protect the environment, and a say in development in the James Bay region. And they wanted money in compensation for what they would give up.

The Inuit, who had less to lose than the Crees because they lived farther from the hydroelectric project, were more accommodating. The key negotiations were between the Crees on one side, and between Quebec and the Energy Corporation on the other.

"It took a little while for the Quebec bureaucrats to get used to [the Crees'] big boots, to their bush clothes" Einar Skinnarland, who was advising the Crees, told me. "The Crees have a sense of humour. When we got down to the nitty gritty, someone would always tell a story."

Skinnarland is a barrel-chested man with an easy laugh and forthright tongue. During World War II, when Germany occupied his native Norway, he was the local contact for the commandos who sabotaged the hydroelectric plant producing heavy water the Germans needed to build their atomic bomb. The leader of the commando team kept a diary which describes a moment one storm-bound morning during the winter of 1942 on the Hardanger plateau, a region of conifer and caribou like that of James Bay. Skinnarland and his comrades had break-fasted on boiled chunks of caribou, chopped from the carcass they kept in a snow bank and, as a vegetable substitute, the green contents of the caribou stomach, rich in Vitamin C. They were crunching on bones, smoking pipes, and drinking coffee. Outside their cabin the snow was blood-stained, and caribou skins, heads, and horns were scattered about. The story of Skinnarland's wartime adventures does not belong here. I mention it only to show that he has lived as the Crees of the James Bay region traditionally did, and this gives him easy rapport with them.[16]

Skinnarland's contribution to the negotiations was to hammer out compromises measured in dollars. "The only thing that counts," he told me, "is money. Whoever has money makes decisions." It was also the style of Armand Couture of Lavalin, chief negotiator on behalf of the Energy Corporation. Between them, they put environmental and social costs into dollars, and traded them against kilowatts. Thus Skinnarland calculated what the flow of water diverted from the Eastmain River was worth to Hydro-Québec, and got half the value of that benefit paid in compensation to the Crees who would lose the river. "The Crees talked like business people once the project became inevitable," Skinnarland told me. "They are unsentimental about the good old days. They would agree to settle for money."

After eight months of negotiation an agreement in principle was struck. Many of the Crees, who were extensively consulted, were reluctant to sign this. Finally in November 1975, after another hectic year of negotiation, racing against a deadline after which the governments' offers would expire, the James Bay and Northern Québec Agreement was signed.

This is a contract by which, in return for surrendering their aboriginal rights and consenting to the hydroelectric project, the Natives got land, self-government, and money.

The Agreement divided just over one million square kilometres of land — not just the James Bay territory, but all of Quebec north of the 49th parallel, that is, two-thirds of the whole province — into three categories. About one percent of this land, in blocks around the villages, is essentially Native-owned. The only resource of interest on this land is wildlife; before the Natives could select land in this category, the provincial government subtracted those areas with known hydroelectric or mineral potential, as well as the land it would need for roads or power lines. About 14 percent of the total area is shared land; only Natives can hunt, trap, and fish here, but Quebec can develop mines, hydroelectric projects, and the like. The remaining 85 percent of the land is public, though certain species of wildlife are reserved for the Natives.

Under the Agreement, the Natives got a kind of regional government. They assumed control of school boards, health and social service boards, and municipal services, for which the federal and provincial governments would pay. They had a voice, with government representatives, on consultative committees set up to protect the environment by reviewing impacts of projects, and on bodies set up to correct damage done to the environment at the La Grande hydroelectric complex.

And they got cash. Hunters were promised a guaranteed minimum annual income. In compensation for the damage done by the hydro-electric project, the Cree communities would receive $135-million over a 20-year period, a payment that amounted to almost $30,000 per person. The Inuit communities received $90-million, or about $20,000 per person.

There have been a number of subsequent amendments and modifications to the James Bay and Northern Québec Agreement.[17] Among these are the Chisasibi Agreement, which allowed the building of the La Grande-1 powerhouse at First Rapids on the La Grande River. For this concession, the Crees received some $60-million with which they paid for their relocation from the sandy island of Fort George to a new village, Chisasibi, built on the shore. Fort George Island is in the estuary of the La Grande River. The Crees feared that it would be washed away by the doubling of the water flow in the river, and some worried that the dams might break. In 1981 many buildings — homes, schools, a chapel and more — were moved from the island, and most of the Crees moved to Chisasibi. Einar Skinnarland managed the relocation for the Crees.

With all these companion agreements, the total compensation paid to the Natives amounts to a little over $500-million, of which about 75 percent has been paid to the Crees. The Natives of northern Quebec now exercise more autonomy that any other Native group in Canada, and control more of the administrative tools designed to protect culture and control development.

Many people and groups, and especially most other Natives, condemn the Crees and Inuit for selling their aboriginal rights. They defend themselves, saying that the fact that the hydroelectric project was being built forced them to sign. The Agreement united the Crees. They ratified it almost unanimously in 1976. It divided the Inuit. About one-fifth of all the Inuit of Quebec refused to authorize the Northern Quebec Inuit Association to negotiate for them, and refused to surrender their aboriginal rights. These dissidents live in Povungnituk and two other villages.[18] These three villages are the cradle and heartland of a vital co-operative movement. It includes shops, hotels, banks, handicraft workshops, and other enterprises. It has encouraged a spirit of self-reliance, aspirations for economic and political independence, and distrust of all bureaucrats, non-Native and Native. Giving up aboriginal rights, the dissident leaders pointed out, meant giving up resources which may be developed, and hence giving up any possibility of economic self-reliance.

For the federal government this was the first treaty signed under the new land claims process and a model precedent. For Quebec, signing the Agreement meant that it fulfilled its obligation to sign a treaty with its northern Natives. It thus strengthened its title to its northern territory and affirmed its jurisdiction there. Many Québécois hailed the Agreement as being generous, open-spirited and innovative, and felt that it ended the colonial relation between Natives and non-Natives. In many ways, the relationship between Quebec and its northern Natives, as codified in the Agreement, resembles that between the British and the French of Canada after the Conquest. In both cases, the minority retained the institutions central to its cultural identity — hunting for the Crees, Catholicism and the French language for the French Canadians — while the majority retained real power. Thus, though the Agreement gave some powers to a Native-run regional government, ultimate power remained in Quebec City.

For the developers, the Agreement was an out-of-court settlement of the Crees' legal actions to stop the James Bay project. Now the developers could continue building the La Grande complex in peace. And now, they believed, the status of the Natives and the rules of the game were defined such that, in the future, they could, without opposition, build more of the James Bay hydroelectric megaprojects.

NOTES

1. Mistissini is also known as Mistassini. In French it is called Baie-du-Porte.
2. Waskaganish (Waskagheganish) was known as Rupert House, and also as Fort Rupert.
3. Hélène Lajambe, interview with author, Montreal, 11 October 1988. (My translation.)
4. Richard Salisbury, interview with author, Montreal, 3 June 1983.
5. Richardson, *Strangers Devour the Land*, 106.
6. John Spence, interview with author, Montreal, 14 March 1984.
7. *The Montreal Gazette*, 8 December 1972. Cited in *A Brief Guide to the James Bay Controversy*, compiled by the Canadian Association in Support of the Native Peoples (April 1973).
8. Einar Skinnarland, interview with author, Montreal, 14 May 1984.
9. Armand Couture, interview with author, La Grande-4, 24 July 1984.
10. See, for instance, the pamphlets *James Bay Development: Progress or disaster*, Le comité pour la défense de la Baie James (Montreal, 1972), and Société pour vaincre la pollution, *La Baie-James: c'est grave, grave, grave* (Éditions Québécoises, 1972).
11. Daniel Green, (President, Société pour vaincre la pollution), interview with author, Montreal, 17 August 1983.
12. Lacasse, *Baie James*, 284.
13. See Jean-Pierre Rogel, *Le paradis de la pollution* (Québec Science, 1983).
14. See Malouf, *La Baie James indienne*.
15. The law favoured the developers too. In November 1974, the Quebec Court of Appeal upheld the appeal of the developers and overturned the Malouf judgement, the application of which it had already suspended.
16. See Thomas Gallagher, *Assault in Norway; Sabotaging the Nazi Nuclear Bomb* (Harcourt, Brace, Jovanovich, 1975): 80. Skinnarland has told me some of his story. In brief, while he maintained radio contact with London, his comrades clambered up the side of a gorge and blew up heavy water stocks and production equipment. The Germans mounted a vast manhunt on the Hardanger plateau. Skinnarland camped on a mountain top. He could see German search parties skiing on the frozen lakes below, but he was never found. Later, when production of heavy water resumed, Skinnarland helped put together another team of saboteurs which blew up a boat carrying railway vans loaded with heavy water. Twenty-six civilian passengers, including women and children, went down with the ship. Skinnarland stayed in the bush, living on the fish he caught and the caribou he shot, until April 1945, when he walked into regional German headquarters, and accepted the surrender of 5,000 German troops and a glass of champagne.
17. Other amendments to the original James Bay and Northern Québec Agreement include the Sakami Lake Agreement, signed in 1979, whereby the community of

Wemindji, for allowing an increase in height of water level in Lakes Sakami, through which water from the diverted Eastmain River flows into the La Grande-2 reservoir, received compensation of $25-million.

18. "Povungnituk" means "where there is a smell of putrefying meat."

CHAPTER 4

Building

Children playing on a beach know intuitively how to pile up embankments to control the routes and rates of downhill-flowing water. The engineers who designed the La Grande hydroelectric complex got to play with the plumbing of a region half the size of Texas, and the techniques they used are elaborate. Nevertheless, although what they did differs in scale and sophistication, it is basically like what children do: they decided where to heap up mounds of dirt.

The amount of power that can be harnessed from a river varies from place to place. It is highest where the flow is heavy, and at rapids or waterfalls, where the river drops sharply. At such sites the designers of hydroelectric projects put dams (which force water to rise and thus, among other things, increase the drop through which it falls), and generating stations (which turn falling water into electricity).

By building a series of dams and generating stations along a river, the designers squeeze power from almost all the vertical distance through which a river drops on its way from source to sea. To squeeze even more power from a river they sometimes swell its flow by diverting neighbouring rivers into it, thus building a hydroelectric complex — a machine whose fuel is running water, and whose key parts are dams and dikes.

Dams and dikes differ only in function. A dam plugs a river in a massive manifestation of human domination of nature. A dike limits the spread of water raised by a dam. In the James Bay region both dams and dikes are made in the same way, of locally-quarried earth materials — these are the first earth dams in Quebec — because shipping concrete this far north would be prohibitively expensive. Moraine, a mixture of sand and pebbles which glaciers ground and dumped, and which is waterproof when compacted, forms the core of the James Bay dams and dikes. Around this core go, first, layers of other earth materials and then, to give the embankment the weight it needs to resist the pressure of the water that pushes against it, a lot of rocks.

Dammed water not only rises but also spreads, forming reservoirs. These have a number of functions. Some, as I have mentioned, increase the height through which water falls at generating stations; these so-called forebay reservoirs are situated upstream of powerhouses. Others, as I shall explain, serve to divert rivers. All serve, primarily, to store water and thus regulate its flow.

In winter, when the land is covered with snow, little water flows in the rivers of northern Quebec. In spring, when the snow melts, the rivers rise dramatically. In autumn, when the rains come, the rivers rise to a smaller peak. With few lakes to smooth out their flow, rivers can be 40 or more times higher during the spring run-off than in winter; these rivers are what hydrologists call flashy.

Like river flow, the amount of electricity Quebec consumes varies markedly with the seasons; but the variation in the demand for power is out of phase with that of river flow, the source of this power. Winter, when river flow is low, is when heat and light are most needed and power consumption peaks. Summer, when river flow is high, is when power consumption is low.

A reservoir stores water when it is available, especially in spring, and releases it when it is needed, especially in winter. Some of the reservoirs in the La Grande complex are so big that they can store water in unusually wet years for use in dry years.

Because the ridges dividing adjacent drainage basins in northern Quebec are low, it is easy, using dams and gravity, to divert water from one river into another. To do so, the engineers first plug a river with a dam higher than the ridge dividing the dammed river from the river into which it is to be diverted. All the water draining the catchment area of the diverted river upstream of the dam will be impounded in a reservoir. As the water in the reservoir rises, it eventually submerges the natural dividing ridge, and flows down the far slope. It is thus diverted. The cut-off dam has become a new height of land, stealing part of one river's catchment area and giving it to another river. On the far slope, the engineers build a second dam as a kind of tap which, when closed, causes the reservoir to fill and, when open, allows the diverted water to flow down its new route.

"How do you divert a river?" I once asked Armand Couture of Lavalin.

"We dam the river," he replied, "and then we throw the impounded waters somewhere else."[1]

Couture was a member of the five-man management committee — Native peoples and the environment were his particular areas of responsibility — which presided over the team of engineers that designed the La Grande complex and managed its construction. This team began to assemble at the Montreal headquarters of the James Bay Energy Corporation in the fall of 1972. A few were employees of the Energy Corporation.

Most were on loan from Hydro-Québec, and from the consulting engineering firms Bechtel and Lavalin.[2]

The La Grande complex, like most artifacts of industrial technology, is not the product of an individual but of a system, one which integrates the knowledge of a number of otherwise ordinary people who have been informed narrowly and deeply, a system which, as Galbraith says, dispenses with the need for genius. The people who designed and built the La Grande complex attended to a myriad details of a multitude of activities. They divided the work to be done into component parts and, since they were in a hurry to get it built, scheduled the sequence in which these should be built so that some components were being constructed before the design of others had been fixed. They engaged consulting engineers to prepare detailed plans and specifications. They awarded bids to contractors to build these components, and supervised the work of the contractors.

The planners built the project on paper many times, with greater detail and improvements in its technical performance at each iteration. They were, they say, optimizing its design — calculating the costs of adding extra metres to the height of a dam, say, and the benefit of the extra kilowatts thereby generated, and choosing the alternative that struck the optimal balance between cost and benefit — that is, the one with the lowest cost per kilowatt generated.

Minimizing production cost was the dominant criterion in designing the La Grande complex. It was because of this, because cheaper was better, and because economies of scale and the topography of the James Bay region dictate that bigger is cheaper, that the James Bay project is so huge. Consider, for example, the design of reservoirs. The planners wanted reservoirs that would stock enough water to run the powerhouses in winter, and that would divert rivers by raising water over divides. In the flat James Bay country, raised water spreads far, forming reservoirs of enormous area. The dikes with which the designers plugged low spots around the rims of reservoirs were intended to contain the reservoirs and define their boundaries, but not, primarily, to limit their area. In planning and optimizing the plan for the La Grande complex, the engineers were not constrained by the areas they were inundating, but only by economics. To the land, lakes, rivers, and wildlife, and to the Natives harvesting these areas, they assigned no value at all.

To decide on the best sites for dams and dikes, to verify the strength of the rock on which these massive structures would rest, to pick the spots at which material from which they would be built would be quarried, to choose the sites for powerhouses, to set the margins of reservoirs and to know how quickly they would fill — to make, in short, a host of decisions, the engineers needed information. When Bourassa launched the project in 1971, Hydro-Québec and its consultants had not completed preliminary studies on the feasibility of a hydroelectric complex in the James Bay region. But the utility had flown several hundred surveyors, geologists, hydrologists and others into exploration camps scattered through the bush. Sleeping under canvas, harassed by bugs, getting around in helicopters or all-terrain vehicles, they were measuring the flow in rivers, mapping the lay of the land, digging and drilling to determine what lay underfoot.

In June 1971, bulldozers and trucks began rolling north from the mining town of Matagami, the nearest point on Quebec's road and rail network to the James Bay wilderness. Pushing down the forest and leveling the land, they were building a road, dirtily but quickly — it advanced at an average rate of more than a kilometre every work day. It was a winter road, its surface the packed snow or, where it crossed rivers, the ice on which, to give extra strength, logs had been laid and flooded.

When this road began, the planners assumed it would end at the Rupert River, which it reached at the end of 1972. But it kept on going north, for the planners by then had chosen not to begin construction of the James Bay project on the southern rivers — that is on the Nottaway,

Broadback, and Rupert, the rivers on which Hydro-Québec had been focusing its studies — but on the La Grande, farther north.

The main reason for this decision was geological. The southern rivers flowed over deep layers of marine clay, deposited on the floor of the seas by melting glaciers. Such clays can turn into a kind of paste when heavy loads are placed on them. Test dikes built in 1971 collapsed. The La Grande River was farther north than the Rupert, and transmitting power from it would therefore be more expensive, but it flowed over the naked rock of the Canadian Shield, rock which could support heavy dams and dikes. (There was another reason, Bourassa disingenuously claimed: the La Grande complex "did not displace any of the Indian communities and left intact the trapping, hunting and fishing areas of the native peoples.")[3]

The La Grande River is well named. It is the third-largest river in Quebec, and the largest flowing into either James Bay or Hudson Bay.[4] The planners chose four of its rapids as sites for powerhouses and dams, and named and numbered these sites, in order of increasing distance from the river's estuary, La Grande-1, La Grande-2, La Grande-3, and La Grande-4. From the highest reservoir, that of LG-4, water would cascade down into the middle reservoir, LG-3, which, in turn, would empty into the lowest reservoir, that of LG-2. (LG-1 was going to be what is called a run-of-the river generating station; it would not have a forebay-reservoir.) Thus the river's profile, in nature a shelving slope, would become a three-step staircase.

Of these four sites, La Grande-2 would provide by far the most power. Here, near the end of its 800-kilometre course across the Quebec-Labrador Peninsula, swollen by almost all its tributaries, the river squeezed through a steep-sided valley and dropped sharply down a tumultuous rapid.

By 1973 the planners had only a tentative scheme for diverting rivers into the La Grande, but they had fixed on it as the central river of the hydroelectric complex, and on LG-2 as the site of its main powerhouse.

While the exploration and optimization continued, work began at LG-2 on what was to become the greatest construction project in the world.

When the road reached the La Grande-2 site in 1973, trucks began rolling north with bulldozers, fuel, food, and building supplies. Bourassa made the long flight north that summer, to celebrate his birthday at La Grande-2 and to rejoice in the racket of hammering, drilling, and blasting. Where once there had been a camp site known to the Crees as "the meeting place," and then a cluster of plywood huts and tents, now workers were building a permanent construction camp, capable of housing thousands, and an airstrip on which jets could land. They were excavating tunnels through which the La Grande would be diverted. They were probing for flaws in the rocks in which the underground generating station would be housed.

Early in 1974, the planners settled on the details of the scheme of diversions and impoundments which has, in the main, been built in phase one of the La Grande complex. They had decided to limit the number of diversions into the La Grande to two so that, they claimed, the flow in its mouth would not increase so much as to wash away the island on which the Cree village of Fort George stood, or so much as to prevent ice, on which the Indians travel, from forming in the estuary. When Bourassa made his first offer to the Natives after the Malouf decision, he claimed that the hydroelectric complex had been redesigned to answer their objections.

Basically, however, the planners' prime criterion was minimizing the unit cost of power; and this, Armand Couture told me, narrowed the choice to eight options. "Making the choice was not easy," he said. "You have to consider the cost of what you don't do, as well as the cost of what you do do...Putting a small plant on a river now, or diverting a portion of the river now, means that you cannot put a large plant on that river later." Because they planned a future complex on the Great Whale River, he explained, they decided not to divert portions of it into the La Grande.

They chose, instead, to divert most of the Eastmain River — along with its tributary, the Opinaca — which flows into James Bay south of the La Grande. In doing so they would create the Opinaca reservoir, which drains through lakes and rivers into the LG-2 reservoir.

They would also divert water from the upper quarter of the basin of the Caniapiscau River, which rises in the centre of the Quebec-Labrador Peninsula, flows north, joins with the Larch to form the Koksoak, and empties into Ungava Bay. Doing so they would create the highest and largest reservoir in the La Grande complex — larger in area than the largest lake in Quebec — and the one whose water level would fluctuate the most — by as much as 13 meters. When they opened the tap at one of the two dams containing the Caniapiscau reservoir, its stored water would pour out, swelling lakes and tributaries of the La Grande, emptying into the LG-4 reservoir, and from there cascading down the dammed La Grande and through its four power-houses. These powerhouses would be capable of producing a maximum of 10,340 megawatts. The two diversions would double the average flow at the mouth of the La Grande, and double its catchment area. There would be five reservoirs — one for each diversion and three along the La Grande — with a total area of 11,335 square kilometres. This is the hydroelectric complex to the construction of which the Crees consented when they signed the James Bay and Northern Québec Agreement.

* * *

At the beginning of the 1974 construction season, a large contingent of workers arrived at La Grande-2. The permanent camp was only half-ready; an early thaw had turned the winter road to mud, bogging down dormitory trailers. Construction materials, food, bedding, all were in short supply. People were crowded. The only way to talk with head-quarters in Montreal was by radio, and reception was often poor. Bad weather often made it impossible to fly into or out of the James Bay region. There was no booze, no women, not even any television, and the rules were strict; anyone fighting or even drinking alcohol, for instance, was fired and put on the next plane south.

This was a time when union power and affluence were growing, especially in construction, the biggest industry in Quebec. Money was flowing into the construction firms that had contracts at James Bay. The unions wanted a slice of the cake too.

Most of the workers at La Grande-2 belonged to unions which, in turn, were affiliated with one or the other of Quebec's two central unions. The largest of these, the Fédération des travailleurs du Québec, (FTQ, the Québec Workers Federation) was pushing to control all workers on the James Bay project. Using intimidation and violence, its representatives were raiding affiliates of its smaller rival, the Confédération des syndicats nationaux (Confederation of National Unions). In March 1974 Laurent Hamel, the La Grande-2 site chief, ex-pelled an FTQ goon for knocking out a worker. The FTQ called a strike, occupying the camp cinema, cafeteria, and Hamel's offices. He and his staff abandoned the camp. Yvon Duhamel, the local FTQ representative, then wrecked the camp. At the controls, first of a crane and then of a loader, Duhamel cut the camp's water pipes, toppled its diesel-fueled generators, and holed its fuel tanks. Fire broke out in the dormitory trailers. Unionized workers were evacuated, by air, from all the James Bay work sites. Construction stopped for some seven weeks.

(A friend of mine, an aircraft mechanic from Paris, was stuck at La Grande-3 with, among others, a chef. They happily cooked their way through fridge-fulls of steak and lobster, exhausting their recipes, and spinning yarns about a bulldozer that the strikers sent off unmanned — it ploughed through bush for 75 kilometres, the story goes, until it finally buried itself beneath an unbudgeable rock.)

During the winter of 1974-1975 a commission enquired into the causes of this riot and, more generally, of violence in Quebec's construction industry.[5] It found, among other things, that Paul Desrochers, Bourassa's principal adviser, was dispensing patronage in the form of jobs at James Bay, and had secretly discussed with the FTQ a scheme to grant it a ten year monopoly on hiring for the hydroelectric project if it would guarantee labour peace. These findings made Bourassa look weak and corrupt, and contributed to his defeat in the provincial election of 1976.

* * *

In 1975, when the James Bay and Northern Québec Agreement was signed, construction was under way throughout the La Grande complex, making it far and away the largest construction site in the world: 1,000 kilometres from east to west, 200 kilometres from north to south. In building this complex industrial civilization colonized wilderness much as plants do; that is, in successive waves, each building on what its predecessors left. Thus the pioneers who arrived at a work site in small planes equipped with skis would shovel enough snow from the ice of a lake to form a temporary runway, large enough for a DC-3 aircraft to land. It would unload a small tractor. With this, the workers could clear a still larger landing strip. The process would continue, culminating in landing strips substantial enough for a giant four-engine Hercules aircraft to land, carrying tons of fuel, or knocked-down cement plants, or almost anything else.

Similarly, the main winter road was succeeded, in October 1974, by a permanent gravel road. Bridges were built, and then this north-south axis was paved. From La Grande-2 the road-builders built an east-west axis, a gravel road which reached the Caniapiscau work site, 725 kilometres to the east, in 1977. It took four days for truckers to get from Matagami, where the Energy Corporation's road network began, to the eastern end of the La Grande complex. It was a gruelling trip. In case of breakdown, the truckers carried survival gear — an axe, dehydrated food, matches, flares — and on arriving at Caniapiscau, some are reported to have burst into tears.

The construction effort swept east, with the road. That is, roughly the same sequence of tasks was being performed at each site, but the farther east the site, the later the sequence began. Thus while the reservoir was filling at LG-2, work was only beginning at Caniapiscau.

The first major task in the sequence by which a hydroelectric plant is built is to create a temporary route for the river to take around the site at which the dam will be constructed. At most of the sites at the La Grande complex, tunnels blasted through the rocky banks of the river provided such a diversion route.

Next, rock is dumped directly into the flowing river from both banks, and the gap through which the water squeezes is narrowed until the river is completely cut off. This pile of rock, a so-called cofferdam, forces the river to rise to the level of the diversion tunnels. Another cofferdam is built downstream of the dam site. When the dam site between these two cofferdams has been pumped dry, and the rocks of the river bed cleaned, wheeled behemoths begin to build the dam.

Enormous shovels, some with buckets big enough to scoop up a family seated round a dinner table, load trucks known as belly-dumpers with rock. Processions of these trucks roll to the dam site, dump their load of more than a hundred tons of rock through the opening in their bellies, and then roll back for another load. Bulldozers and compactors move the dumped material and shape the dam.

Next, the sluice gates on the diversion tunnels are closed, and the tunnels permanently sealed with concrete plugs. The reservoir starts to fill. In 1978, when the La Grande-2 reservoir began to fill, the water rose 15 meters in the first day. About a year later, the reservoir was full.

If a reservoir were to overflow it could destroy its dam — the worst catastrophe the planners can imagine. To prevent this happening, spillways are built, drains through which surplus water can, when necessary, be safely discharged. The La Grande-2 spillway is a long, canyon-like staircase blasted out of the rock, big enough to carry all the flow of the mighty Saint Lawrence River as it sweeps around the island of Montreal, and more.

Next, the powerhouses. At La Grande-2, two huge underground caverns, and many tunnels, have been blasted out of solid rock. The principle cavern is for the machine hall. From the reservoirs, water drops through conduits called penstocks, down to the steel scroll cases which spiral around the turbines like the shell of a nautilus, and then swirls through the turbines, forcing their runners to turn. The runners are coupled to the rotors of the generators mounted above them.

Like alternators in cars, the rotors spin inside coils which counteract their spinning with electromagnetic forces. The greater the load on the grid, the greater these forces. Driven by the falling water, the rotors spin against these forces, generating electricity.

Transformers in the switchyards above the powerhouses increase the voltage at which this electricity is generated to the very high levels used for long-distance transmission, and the power flows south, through the lines looping from towers marching over the land, through the switching stations with their circuit breakers, transformers, capacitor banks, and the other heavy electrical equipment that regulates its flow.

The second cavern at the LG-2 powerhouse is the surge chamber, into which, after spinning the turbines, the waters pour. This chamber functions as a pressure damper; here, when turbines are shut down or started up, the energy of the water falling into the powerhouse is dissipated safely. On a rack near the entrance to the surge chamber there are rows of lifejackets. Inside, the air is chill and damp. You can venture the length of the chamber on a high catwalk. It feels like a prison, a place where force is subdued. Far below, most of its energy spent, flows the mingled water of the La Grande, the Eastmain, and the Caniapiscau Rivers.

* * *

After the rampage at LG-2 in 1974, the Energy Corporation instituted a far-reaching system of social control. On arriving at the project everybody was photographed and issued an identity card, by means of which his or her whereabouts was tracked. No one could enter the James Bay territory without the corporation's permission. It controlled transport, communications, housing, everything. The entire social order in this great domain existed for the work.

At the peak of construction, in 1978 and 1979, there were some 20,000 people on the James Bay work sites, and more than 2,000 to the south, building power lines. At the work sites, most slept two to a room in 12-room dormitory trailers. (Management personnel lived in bungalows in their own villages, apart from the workers.) Workers rose early, had breakfast in the hangar-like cafeteria, chose lunch from the ample supplies on the self-service counter, and began work at seven in the morning. Twelve hours later, they had supper in the cafeteria.

Services improved greatly after the rampage. There were post offices, bars, banks, television, leisure centres, gymnasia, weight-lifting rooms, bowling alleys, swimming pools, ping pong, photography studios, arenas for hockey in winter, tennis in summer, cinemas. Some grew as dependent on the system here as prisoners grow on that of a prison. They liked being fed, heated, housed, and entertained; they liked the intense social relations that develop in such small and isolated communities. Others found the regimentation and security suffocating, boring and unprivate. Many avoided the leisure centres, the hockey games and beauty pageants and limbo competitions and amateur variety shows. They had not come to Baie James to have fun, but to be drugged by long hours of work, and to make money.

Rates of pay at the James Bay project were only slighter higher than standard rates in Quebec, but workers made more than they could elsewhere by working long hours and collecting overtime. With overtime, unskilled workers could earn $30,000 or $35,000 per year, twice what they could in the city, and save much of it. The workers had no expenses, for the Energy Corporation fed, housed, and entertained them. Many saved, so they could build or buy houses without borrowing, or start small businesses, or buy boats, or motorbikes.

Twenty-six lives were lost in constructing phase one of the La Grande complex — a good safety record. Workers there told me apocryphal stories of live burials, of cranes toppling with their operators into damp concrete, never to be seen again — in this mild form, as stories told to elicit a shudder of fear, the ancient tradition of propitiating a river with a human sacrifice when building a bridge or dam still lingers.

Marcel Paré, a biologist, told me of a death he witnessed while counting caribou. It was mid-October, and the weather was bad: rainy, snowy, windy. He and another wildlife biologist, Danielle Perron, decided that she would remain in their helicopter which, flying low and slow, would drive some caribou out of the trees in which they were sheltering. Paré and an assistant waited on the ground to count them. A sudden gust of wind caught the chopper. It spun around one and half times, falling. As it hit ground, Danielle jumped out. She was not running away from danger, the pilot must have known, but into it, for helicopters rarely explode. He ran after her, to stop her. When Paré and his companion reached the crash site, the rotor blades were still turning. They had severed the pilot's head from his torso, and struck Diane a lethal blow on the ear.

In 1978 the planners redesigned the La Grande complex once again. They chose to build it in two phases, to complete only the three most profitable powerhouses, LG-2, LG-3, and LG-4, leaving LG-1, and other elements, for a second phase.[6] In 1984, just before phase one of the La Grande complex was complete, I went for a walk at LG-4 with John Spence. The wind was cool and carried the scent of spruce. Fireweed bloomed in the clearings near the camp. In the distance, where water cascaded over the spillway, mist rose like smoke from soundless explosions. As we tramped along the dirt road, the roar of falling water grew louder. We passed under power lines, buzzing and crackling with electricity and, at the foot of the spillway, watched water cascading down from the reservoir, shooting up the lip of an immense, concrete ski jump, then falling into the pool below.

"What an achievement," Spence said. "I was here ten years ago, and I wouldn't have believed it could have been done. It was superbly organized. Maybe it was not built at the right place, or at the right time, or at the right rhythm, but it's a magnificent achievement nonetheless."

The following year, the Energy Corporation handed the completed complex over to Hydro-Québec to run. Camps, houses, offices, communities — almost all were temporary, built to be struck like stage sets, and trucked away. The people who had worked here, and the hundreds of thousands of tons of fuel, of food, and of explosives were gone. Behind them they left some 1,600 kilometres of roads, five airports, thousands of kilometres of high-voltage power lines, and hundred of millions of cubic meters of dirt, piled into synthetic mountains, the collective product of politicians' schemes, engineers' calculations, and labourers' sweat.

According to the Energy Corporation, to build phase one of the La Grande complex, including the cost of the associated power lines, cost almost $16-billion, about double the original estimates. (Others estimate the cost as being as high as $20-billion.) Though not technically as challenging as the United States's Apollo project, the per capita cost, for Quebecers, was 15 times greater than that, for Americans, of their venture to the Moon.[7]

Because of this project, a handful of operators in Montreal can, with ease comparable to that of children playing with puddles, choreograph the rise and fall of great volumes of water in the sub-Arctic, and transform the movement of this water into electricity.

NOTES

1. Armand Couture, interview with author, La Grande-4, 24 July 1984.
2. To be precise, it was Lalonde, Valois, Lamarre, Valois et Associés, a subsidiary of the holding company Lavalin Inc., which co-managed with Bechtel International the building of phase one of the La Grande complex.
3. Bourassa, *James Bay*, 59.
4. River size, in this comparison, is measured by drainage basin area. That of the La Grande River, before it was harnessed, was 98,000 square kilometres.
5. Brian Mulroney, now Prime Minister of Canada, first became known to the general public as a member of this, the Cliche Commission.
6. The main reason for doing this was to meet Hydro-Québec's growing need for peak power. This, in turn, was largely due to the growing use of electricity for home-heating; all the heaters in Quebec are drawing power at the same time in mid-winter. To increase the power capacity of the La Grande complex, the planners installed more generators in powerhouses. This meant that water — which represents potential energy — could be drawn down from the reservoirs faster than previously planned. It did not change the amount of energy the complex could generate in a year. Lowering the capacity factor, as this change is technically called, means that the generating units will be idle for a greater fraction of the year than was originally planned. It also meant that the reservoirs will fluctuate more wildly.
7. Morisset, *L'Identité usurpée*, 151.

CHAPTER 5

Selling

In the November 1976 provincial elections, René Lévesque led the Parti Québécois to an unexpected victory over Bourassa and the Liberals. The new government had promised to seek public consent for its project of making Quebec independent, and at this prospect, in the words of balladeer Felix Leclerc, "six-million bosoms resounded with joy."

No political party likes to continue its predecessor's program, but the Parti Québécois, which had opposed the James Bay project, now supported it. "Only fools never change their minds," Lévesque explained, and Guy Joron, the first Parti Québécois energy minister, called Bourassa's decision to build the project "the best bad decision ever made."[1] It was bad because it led to a project that was built too big and too soon, and that was tainted by partisan politics. It was good because the cartel of oil-producing nations jacked up the price of oil by a factor of ten during the 1970s, creating a new market for Quebec's electricity that no one could have predicted. Between 1976 and 1985, the years during which the Parti Québécois was in power and the first phase of the La Grande complex was being completed, Quebec became a major exporter of electricity to northeast America — a surprising development for a province which had been isolated not only culturally but also electrically.

The search for profits leads most electric utilities in the industrial world to expand their grids of power lines and to link their grids together into integrated networks.[2] To understand why this is so, consider the balance between supply and demand for electric power. A utility must be able to supply enough power to meet its load — the power demanded at any moment by all the customers plugged into its grid. Loads fluctuate. Hydro-Québec's load, for instance, rises to a peak early every evening, when most of its two and a half million customers come home from work, cook dinner, and bathe the kids. It rises to an annual peak on mid-winter evenings, when people also switch on lights and heaters. The power a utility supplies must vary to match its load. The capacity of a utility, the total power it can supply, must be at least big enough to meet its annual peak load. As the load drops below peak, some of a utility's capacity becomes, temporarily, surplus to its needs. Hydro-Québec has a large surplus of power in the summer, when run-off from rivers in Quebec is high.

Utilities do not like to have their power plants standing idle and not making money. One way for a utility to minimize its surpluses is to expand the area it serves, and thus the number of its customers. The more customers it has plugged into its grid, the more diversity there is likely to be among the uses of power which combine to shape its load, and the less likely it is that customers will all want power at the same time. Increasing diversity reduces fluctuations in load, and thus reduces temporary surpluses.

Seeking diversity, then — and the advantages of economies of scale — utilities tend to expand the areas their grids cover, from cities to regions. When a utility can no longer expand because it bumps into another utility, both then tend to link up, forming what are called power pools. The New York Power Pool, for example, integrates the eight electrical utilities which handle almost all electricity in New York State. Similarly, the New England Power Pool integrates more than 60 utilities in its region. By linking together, utilities enjoy mutual benefits. A utility which happens to need power can buy it from another which happens to have a temporary surplus. (This is called a diversity exchange.) A utility which happens to be able to generate relatively low-cost power can sell it to another, which thus avoids having to generate power at higher cost at one of its power plants. (This is called an economy exchange.) Mutual reliability is improved, for when one utility has a breakdown it can draw power from its neighbours.

By the 1970s, this process of expansion and integration led to major connections between the United States and Canada. Two integrated super-grids now covered (and cover) most of North America: the Western Interconnection, centred on Los Angeles, which tapped power from as far away as Western Canada and Mexico; and the Eastern Interconnection, which linked thousands of power plants east of the Rockies. Quebec, however, was largely isolated from its electrical neighbours.

Everything in a grid — generators, power lines, switching stations, loads — is connected, and the effect of anything that happens is felt simultaneously everywhere else. The dynamics of massive flows of power through such richly interactive systems are extremely complex, and difficult to control.

Most power in North America is carried by alternating current. In such a current electric charges flow first in one direction, then the other, alternating at a frequency of 60 cycles per second. (Everywhere in the industrial world, sensitive acoustic apparatus can pick up the low tone sounded by alternating current.) A synchronized grid is one throughout which this frequency is constant, and the voltage waves driving the alternating current are in phase.[3] Changes in the load — and loads continually change — tend to change the frequency and phase in a grid. So, too, do power lines: the longer they are, the more they distort the power passing through them. Automatic feedback systems strive to compensate for such changes, to keep all the generators feeding a grid turning together, to keep frequency and phase everywhere constant — in a word, to keep the grid synchronized.

In Quebec, power lines are extraordinarily long. Those linking the James Bay project to Montreal are 1,100 kilometres in length, and those from Churchill Falls are even longer. The routes are few but the lines are long, so long that in total length, Hydro-Québec's high-voltage transmission network exceeds that of any other utility in the world.

The challenge of synchronizing this hugely elongated grid pushes technology to its limits. Picture a grid as a group of heavy pendulums swinging in unison, and linked together by fragile threads. When one pendulum loses the beat, the threads snap. That is, if something disturbs the flow of power through Quebec's grid — such as a power line collapsing under the weight of ice, or a transformer blowing up, or lightning or solar flares causing power surges — and if the control systems fail to stabilize the grid, the grid crashes, and the province plunges into a blackout. During the 1970s, Quebec's grid crashed more than once a year, on average. Between 1970 and 1991 it has crashed 11 times, and there have been thousands of smaller failures.

Such breakdowns can flow through linked grids as easily as power. In 1965, a momentary overload in the Ontario Hydro grid caused cascading failures throughout the Northeast, and left some 30 million people either in the dark, jammed in elevators, stuck in subway cars, snarled in traffic, or otherwise mired in what the *New Yorker* called a "festival of inconvenience."

Quebec's neighbours are understandably reluctant to risk importing blackouts along with power. "Connecting Quebec with the Northeast is like holding two elephants together with a rubber band," an American utility engineer has said. "You have problems when one of them wiggles, and elephants wiggle a lot."[4]

Nonetheless, there are at least two compelling reasons for utilities in the Northeast to connect with Quebec. The first is the potential for diversity exchanges. Quebec has a surplus when the East coast megalopolis has most need for power: in summer, when the air conditioners in Boston and New York are running at full blast. Early in the 1970s, Hydro-Québec regularly exploited this seasonal diversity by exporting small quantities of surplus power, mainly via Ontario to New York. This power came from a hydroelectric station near Montreal, at which Hydro-Québec disconnected several generators from its own grid and synchronized them with the Ontario and New York grids.

The second reason is the possibility for a one-way economy exchange. Utilities in the Northeast are heavily dependent on oil: in the late 1970s, as much as a third of the electricity in New York state, and an even larger fraction in New England, came from oil-fired power plants. Oil was soaring in cost and unreliable in supply. Hydro-Québec — like other Canadian utilities — was willing to sell its surplus electricity at an attractive price: 80 percent of the cost of the electricity generated at oil or coal-fired plants in the United States.

Hydro-Québec entered this electricity export business with a bang in 1978: it built an interconnection through which the Power Authority of the State of New York (known now as the New York Power Authority, NYPA), a utility owned by the state government, began directly importing surplus power and energy from Quebec, for resale to other members of the New York Power Pool.

* * *

Hydro-Québec's surpluses increased dramatically when power began to flow south from James Bay. In October 1979 the La Grande-2 powerhouse was inaugurated in the first and splashiest of the celebrations held to mark the completion of components of phase one of the La Grande complex. For many Québécois, this inauguration was an occasion for self-congratulation. The builders of something truly big in North America were, for the first time, *not* Anglo-Saxons — the ethnic label under which Quebec nationalists lump all English-speaking North Americans — but French. No longer did Saint Jean-Baptiste's docile lamb epitomize the Québécois, one orator declaimed as the week long celebration drew to a close, but masterful dam builders, who were launching pylons to carry Light as far south as the Statue of Liberty. The La Grande-2 powerhouse, said René Lévesque, who presided over the culminating ceremony, could produce, for all eternity, a flow of electricity equivalent in energy content to a flow of 150 thousand barrels of oil a day. He pulled a switch. Power began to flow south.

Billy Diamond and other Native leaders had turned down invitations to attend the ceremony. Bourassa had not. He had suffered a humiliating defeat in 1976; voters had seen him as a wimp, sneering at accounts of his ever-present sidekick, a gun-toting bodyguard-cum-hairdresser. Legislation he had introduced limiting the use of English was unpopular — in the case of English-speaking voters, because it restricted their liberties; in the case of Québécois, because it was not tough enough to protect the French language. Bourassa had disappeared from public life. But now, at the inauguration of La Grande-2, he reappeared. He was not a prominent member of the official party, but he upstaged Lévesque; the workers remembered Bourassa and welcomed him loudly as the father of the James Bay project. Here, at La Grande-2, Bourassa began to climb back to power.

He continued this climb during the referendum campaign the following year, when Quebecers got to vote on whether or not to give to the

Lévesque government a mandate to negotiate independence — or, rather, sovereignty-association. Bourassa campaigned for the "*Non*" vote. Maybe the wit is right who said that what Quebecers really want is an independent Quebec in a strong Canada. A majority of the six million Quebecers voted "No" in the 1980 referendum, quashing, for a while, the hopes of the *indépendantistes* to realize their dream. Lévesque was heartbroken but still hopeful. "*À la prochaine fois*" (until next time), he said to his disappointed supporters.

Ironically, both Lévesque and Bourassa, in their referendum speeches, invoked the James Bay project. For Lévesque, it was a symbol of political autonomy to come. For Bourassa, it was a promise of economic autonomy, a first step on the path that would turn Quebec into one of the wealthiest societies in North America.

In his view, rivers are raw materials which can be turned into a commodity: electricity. By leaving its wild rivers wild, Quebec was wasting energy. It should dam its rivers. In his 1981 book *Deux fois la Baie James* (James Bay Twice), he proposed that Quebec capture another 25,000 megawatts, doubling the power harnessed in the first phase of the La Grande complex. Quebec should sell electricity where it fetched the highest price: that is, in the states of New England and New York, an enormous, accessible, and potentially lucrative market.

Though his logic leads to the conclusion that Quebec should build power plants solely to generate power for export, Bourassa has never suggested this. To do so is politically unacceptable: how could Quebec hope to remain in any degree autonomous if the world's dominant power depended heavily and permanently on its hydroelectricity? What Bourassa proposed, rather, was that Quebec build now the power plants it was going to need to meet future demand. Hydro-Québec, at the beginning of the 1980s, forecast continuing high growth, growth so dizzy that to meet it all of Quebec's rivers would have to be dammed by the turn of the century. Do it now, said Bourassa. Create a year-round surplus of at least

10,000 megawatts, and export it to the United States. In paying for the power under long-term contracts, the Americans would pay off the loans made to finance the new power plants.

Bourassa acknowledged, in passing, that some Americans might object to new power lines, but he was confident they would see that importing electricity would reduce pollution by reducing the fuel burned at American power plants. To the concerns of Native peoples or of environmentalists in Quebec, he did not even pay lip service.

Hydro-Québec's president — Robert Boyd, former president of the James Bay Energy Corporation — and many of its senior managers were uncomfortable with the mercantile role Bourassa envisioned for them. Hydro-Québec, they believed, should continue supplying electricity to Quebecers at the lowest possible cost, and furthering Quebec's industrial development. The utility's mandate, in fact, prohibited it from exporting anything other than temporary surpluses.

But at least one cadre shared Bourassa's vision. Jacques Guevremont, a tall, slightly stooped engineer, was then Hydro-Québec's vice-president for production and transport. In January 1981, he told a group of contractors that although the utility was not thinking of building power plants dedicated to export, it might build projects before Quebec needed their output in order sell firm electricity to the United States.[5]

"Offering to sell electricity is like offering to sell citrus fruit." Guevremont told me once. "You want to know whether it is oranges, lemons or grapefruit you're talking about — that is, is the product surplus energy, firm energy, or firm capacity?"[6] There are two distinctions to be made here: between energy, the capacity to do work, and power, the rate at which work is done; and between interruptible contracts, under which delivery can be reduced or stopped at any time, and firm contracts, which guarantee delivery of specified quantities of energy, or power, for specified periods of time. Surplus energy being, by nature, temporary, it is sold only when available under interruptible contracts.

Firm contracts entail more binding obligations. Firm capacity refers to power that is available all the time. The selling utility undertakes to pay a penalty if it fails to keep its promises. The purchasing utility promises to pay even if it does not take delivery of the energy or use the power capacity.

Firm contracts, and especially firm capacity contracts, involve commitments that last for decades. A contract guaranteeing an American utility that it can draw, say, 1,000 megawatts of power from Hydro-Québec at any time without interruption is equivalent to a new power plant, and it allows the purchasing utility to postpone building a new plant, or to mothball a plant that generates electricity expensively.

What was enticing Hydro-Québec — and other Canadian utilities — to export firm electricity was the quandary facing American utilities. They anticipated building new power plants, as in the past, to meet growth in demand and to replace aging facilities. But, especially in the Northeast, they now faced formidable barriers to building. Construction of more oil-fired plants would be folly, given the price of oil. The public had rejected nuclear power, and the billions poured into such plants as Shoreham in Long Island and Seabrook in New Hampshire were being written off as bad investments. People were reluctant to accept coal-burning plants, because they pollute the atmosphere. Raising capital for any kind of plant was hard, as was satisfying the regulators and meeting environmental criteria. How much easier it would be to import firm electricity from Hydro-Québec; not only easier, but clean, sure, and cheap. Running water is the most environmentally benign natural source from which to tap energy, and any damage done is done in the remote wilds of northern Quebec, out of sight and mind of electricity consumers in the Northeast. There are no unknowns about hydroelectric technology. Canadian reluctance to sign contracts for the long periods Americans preferred — of 15 to 30 years — had scuttled earlier import schemes. But now that Hydro-Québec had enormous surpluses, it was happy to make long term commitments, and to sell its electricity cheaply.

* * *

The world-wide recession at the beginning of the 1980s hit hard in Quebec. Businesses were failing, people losing their jobs. Because of this, and because of conservation stimulated by rising prices for energy, the demand for electricity in Quebec stopped growing as quickly as the forecasters had predicted it would. In 1982, in fact, it actually shrank. At the same time, phase one of the La Grande complex was nearing completion, adding huge amounts of power to Quebec's capacity. Hydro-Québec's surpluses, in consequence, were enormous, even in winter. In 1985, Hydro-Québec's capacity (including the output of Churchill Falls) exceeded its mid-winter peak demand by about 7,000 megawatts, and it expected to have surpluses until the end of the decade.

Yet in 1981, as this gross imbalance between supply and demand developed, Hydro-Québec still forecast that demand would double every decade and, to meet future demand, it still planned to complete the James Bay project— first the second phase of the La Grande complex and Great Whale complex, then the Nottaway-Broadback-Rupert complex — by century's end.

In 1981, when Parti Québécois politicians challenged Hydro-Québec's optimistic forecast, the ongoing struggle for power between the government of Quebec and its utility became, briefly, visible. The government was trying to get the utility to implement the Parti Québécois policy of stimulating consumption of electricity within Quebec, and thus increasing the degree to which the province would be powered by its own energy resources. As well, the government needed money to finance its expensive social programs; it needed to create jobs. Hydro-Québec was an instrument it could use to achieve all these ends, for the utility controls much of the flow of money through the Quebec economy. The government tried, in a number of ways, to reduce Hydro-Québec's autonomy. In 1981, Quebec began tapping Hydro-Québec's cash flow. Since then, when the utility makes a profit, it pays a dividend to its sole shareholder, the government. In January 1982 the government appointed as chief executive officer of Hydro-Québec someone who, for the first time, was *not* one of the utility's engineers.

Guy Coulombe was an experienced administrator — he had held some of the highest posts in the Quebec civil service. He was sensitive to the Parti Québécois' program, and he had a mind of his own. "Realizing that we were heading for a crisis with the recession just around the bend," he has said, "I was convinced that, given the drop in demand, the construction program was ridiculously ambitious. Hydro-Québec was a firm of engineers whose ultimate goal was to build dams. I knew that if we didn't stop that, we were heading for bankruptcy."[7]

Hydro-Québec did not stop construction of the first phase of the La Grande complex; even though its output would swell the surplus, to finish the complex was cheaper than to postpone it. But, with Coulombe at the helm, Hydro-Québec dropped its forecast of load growth from around seven percent per year to less than three percent, and postponed the planned start of construction on the rest of the James Bay project. Jacques Parizeau, then the Parti Québécois' Minister of Finance, wanted more hydro construction as a way of creating jobs, but Coulombe argued that "it's not going to help the economy if Hydro-Québec goes to the devil." The utility reduced its investment program, and rather than spending money on new construction, spent it on improvements to its grid. "It's more complicated to reduce black-outs by ten percent on the grid," Coulombe said, "than to build LG-4."[8]

Meanwhile, because there was no market for the power it could generate, water was cascading down the spillways of the La Grande complex. "We had 30 billion kilowatthours we couldn't sell [in 1983],"

Coulombe told a reporter. "For this we're going to build more dams, just so the water can spill over the edge? It's perhaps majestic to look at, but who's going to pay for it?"[9]

Hydro-Québec began aggressively selling its surplus electricity both within Quebec and in the United States. To make sales it had to sell cheaply, for there was a glut of electricity on the market. But the utility calculated that even selling electricity for less than its production cost brought in something, whereas spilled water brought in nothing at all.

Within Quebec, residential and commercial markets were virtually saturated with electricity. The proportion of homes heated by electricity in Quebec had been rising dramatically, for instance, and almost all new houses in Quebec are electrically heated.

There was, however, the possibility of increasing sales by offering cut rates to industries, such as the aluminum refining industry, that voraciously consume electricity. Electric fields strong enough to erase credit cards, stop digital watches, or pull a wrench from your hands are what separate pure aluminum from its ore. An aluminum smelter uses as much power as a small city. So much electricity is used in making it that aluminum can be thought of as congealed electricity; the multinational firms who produce aluminum build their billion-dollar smelters not where the ore is mined, but where they can be assured of getting abundant, cheap electricity. Hydro-Québec offered rates low enough to induce several of these firms, notably Reynolds and Péchiney, to build or expand aluminum smelters in the Saint Lawrence Valley, and to induce other firms to build a magnesium smelter, and pulp and paper mills. All these plants use enormous quantities of electricity and, since their products are mainly exported, they are, in effect, exporting Quebec's electricity.

* * *

Eager to escape the limitations of its domestic market, Hydro-Québec also began a push to sell electricity to the United States. At the end of 1982, Georges Lafond, who had been negotiating the utility's loans, took a newly-created position, that of vice-president for external markets. Jacques Guevremont, who formally became the utility's chief negotiator of export deals at that time, had already negotiated a big one — an interruptible contract to ship greatly increased quantities of seasonal surpluses to the New York Power Authority. In June 1983, the Parti Québécois government changed Hydro-Québec's mandate, allowing it to export firm power under long term contracts, to behave like a commercial enterprise.

To become a big exporter, Hydro-Québec needed to overcome its electrical isolation. It began building an interconnection with New England, and expanding its interconnection with New York State. By using recent advances in the technology of direct current transmission in these interconnections, it was gearing up to send massive power flows to its neighbours' grids, without risk of desynchronizing them.

The electric current in the early electric power systems was direct current — so-called because it flows without changing direction. Thomas Edison, the inventor of the first power system, fought unscrupulously against the introduction of alternating current. Direct current is safe, he pointed out, but alternating current kills, and he demonstrated this by electrocuting dogs and cats, and by campaigning — successfully — for the installation of the first electric chair in a New York prison. Edison lost the battle, however, because — among other reasons — the technology needed to transmit direct current over long distances did not exist in his time.

Only by raising voltages considerably above those used in homes — by light bulbs and other devices — can electricity be transmitted any distance without major loss of energy. The transformer, invented at the beginning of this century, readily raises and lowers voltages in alternating current circuits. But, until the middle of this century, there was no comparable device for changing voltages in direct current circuits. Since then, solid state devices have been invented that readily convert alternating current to direct current, and back again. It is these developments that have ended Quebec's electrical isolation. By exporting power though direct current — which, since it does not alternate, has no frequency — Hydro-Québec avoids exporting instability.

Hydro-Québec installed its first direct current interconnection in 1984: a so-called back-to-back direct current buffer in the sub-station from which it exports power to New York. Alternating current power drawn from the Quebec grid — and synchronized with it — enters the station and is converted to direct current. After a very short run within the station, it is converted back into alternating current — now synchronized with the New York grid, into which it then flows. In March 1982, Hydro-Québec agreed to ship greatly increased quantities of its seasonal surpluses under interruptible contracts to the New York Power Authority through this interconnection.[10]

New England was also a promising market for Hydro-Québec. There is the same seasonal complementarity in load between Boston and Montreal as there is between New York City and Montreal; and New England was even more heavily reliant on oil than New York state — in the early 1980s more than half of all the electricity generated in New England came from oil-fired plants.

In 1983 Hydro-Québec signed the first phase of a complex two-phase cluster of agreements with the New England Power Pool. Phase one included a deal to sell blocks of both interruptible power and energy,[11] and to build a direct current power line linking a Hydro-Québec sub-station with a substation in New Hampshire. As part of phase two of this deal, signed in October 1985, the direct current line is being extended. The sixth power line from the James Bay project, it runs some 2,500 kilometres from La Grande-2 to the vicinity of Boston.

In July 1984, Hydro-Québec signed its first deal to export firm power year round, with Vermont.[12] The second phase of its deal with the New England Power Pool, signed the following year, included a firm commitment to export a large block of energy. Hydro-Québec was going to be supplying about ten percent of New England's electricity during the 1990s.[13]

By 1985, Hydro-Québec's salesmen had unloaded much of its surplus power on the interruptible market, selling huge quantities at less than production cost. (The fact that Hydro-Québec was buying power from Churchill Falls for even less than it charged its American customers helped.) Hydro-Québec was rapidly outselling its competition and becoming the biggest Canadian exporter of electricity.

"Exports are going to increase very dramatically," Guevremont told me in 1984. "But after that they will come to an end. When the contracts for firm power which we hope to sign end — around 2010, 2015 — they will not be renewed. We will need the power we generate internally. Our neighbours will have to build. Hydroelectricity from Quebec is in other words a transition energy source, something they can use now, deferring investment they otherwise would have to make, buying time to plan the future."

Why did American utilities not conserve energy rather than buy from Hydro-Québec? Guevremont shrugged expressively. Hard-nosed businessmen from the New England Power Pool had considered and rejected that option, in favour of buying from Hydro-Québec.

Like highways, the interconnections invited further traffic. The Hydro-Québec salesmen were negotiating new, bigger, firmer, and longer-term deals. Hydro-Québec, forced to export because it had a surplus, became interested in creating surpluses in order to export. Guevremont showed me a map of the rivers which Hydro-Québec was planning to harness. The Great Whale complex was scheduled to be in operation in the year 2000. "Our clients," he said, "don't care where we build. All they care about is the price."[14]

NOTES

1. *Le Soleil* (Quebec City), 16 June 1976; Guy Joron, "Interview. Une priorité: Le respect de nos ressources énergétiques," *Forces* 48 (1978): 18-32.
2. See Hughes, *Networks of Power*.
3. Alternating current is transmitted in three separate voltage waves known as phases. The voltages in each phase are identical in all respects except for timing. The peak of the first voltage wave arrives 1/180th of a second (one third of a cycle) before that of the second, and the second wave lags behind the third by the same amount of time. Each of the three bundles of conductors in a high-voltage power line carries a separate phase. Stability in a grid requires constancy both of frequency and of phase relations.
4. Jane Kramer, "Power-full ties link Canada, United States," *Focus: Views on Energy* (Consumers Power Company, Michigan) (4,2): 9-15.
5. See André Delisle, "Le Mirage des Hydro-Dollars," *Québec-Science* (April 1982): 42-47.
6. Jacques Guevremont, interview with author, Montreal, 3 July 1984.
7. Bombardier, "Guy Coulombe." (My translation.)
8. *La Presse* (Montreal), 10 March 1984. (My translation.)
9. Hadekel, "Power Play," 23.
10. Under this deal the New York Power Authority contracted to buy up to 111 terawatthours of interruptible surplus energy from Hydro-Québec during the 13 year period from 1984 to 1997, and to make seasonal imports of 1,200 megawatts of firm power until 1992. (A terawatthour equals a billion kilowatthours.)
11. Up to 33 terawatthours of energy during an 11 year period.
12. 150 megawatts of firm, year-round capacity, and a maximum of 1.3 terawatthours per year.
13. In phase two of its contract with Hydro-Québec, the New England Power Pool contracted to buy seven terawatthours of firm energy every year for ten years beginning in 1990. Due to delays in constructing the direct current power line linking the La Grande complex to the New England grid, only two terawatthours were delivered in 1990-1991.
14. Jacques Guevremont, interview with author, Montreal, 3 July 1984.

CHAPTER 6

Changing Nature

"Present, yet leaving no trace..." the James Bay Energy Corporation proclaims in a number of glossy brochures, flattering itself on its care for the environment in building the La Grande complex. The photographs in these brochures belie the words. Some show heavy machinery dumping dirt on the taiga. Others, taken from the air, show vast expanses of sky, forest, and water, all seemingly untouched by civilization — until the viewer realizes how much life was drowned by the spreading water.

In 1983, when the Caniapiscau reservoir was still filling, I talked to a party of canoeists who had just paddled across the huge body of shallow water. They described their paddle tips brushing spruce candles, brushing the tops of trees which, though drowned, still reached for life.

No comprehensive assessment of anticipated impacts was made before the bulldozers began moving earth at the La Grande complex.

Concerns about its environmental and social effects failed to stop it, to slow it, or to modify its basic design. True, when the planners could choose between two design options, both of which satisfied their prime criterion — that of squeezing electricity from rivers at minimum unit cost — they chose the least damaging option: where, for instance, they could choose between two valleys, they drowned the less biologically productive one. But the essential features of the project were fixed without thought for its effects on nature and people.

The Energy Corporation claims to have "inserted the hydroproject as harmoniously as possible into the environment." In translating the plans for the project into reality, the corporation evinced some sensitivity to environmental and social concerns. Driving from the airport to the dam at La Grande-2, for instance, you can see land which the road builders stripped of vegetation and soil. Thanks to the application of a lot of fertilizer and the planting of many bushes and trees, growing greenery now veils this land. This image captures the essence of the environmental policy of the James Bay Energy Corporation — and of its owner, Hydro-Québec: first build, then paint green.

According to a former director of the Energy Corporation's environment department, what "forced the administrators...to take the environmental aspect into account" was the political struggle against the James Bay project.[1] To controvert its critics, in other words, and to establish a public image of a corporation that cares, the James Bay Energy Corporation became the first company in Quebec, and one of the first in Canada, to have an environment department. Of the traces the Energy Corporation has left, the most obvious are physical changes to the environment, and the most visible of these are the reservoirs. As the water rose in the reservoirs of the La Grande complex, it submerged, first, the banks of streams and lakes. Here, fed by nutrients carried by the spring flood a diverse community of plants such as alder and willow flourished. These plants sheltered and fed beaver, muskrat, snowshoe hare, otter, shore birds, and other animals. This zone, where water and land overlap, is the most biologically productive in the James Bay region. The rising water drowned in total some 83,000 kilometres of such natural shorelines, and in doing so inflicted what is probably the most severe of its impacts on nature. It drowned campsites and graves of the Crees who, for millennia, have traveled and hunted, lived and died along these river valleys. As the water continued to rise, it drowned some 12,000 square kilometres of forest.

Water level in the reservoirs fluctuates according to electricity demand, and thus follows a cycle that is almost the inverse of the natural cycle. Water now falls in winter, when the demand for electricity rises (the La Grande-2 reservoir, for instance, drops seven meters in winter) and rises in summer as the demand falls. The drawdown zone, the area between the high and low water marks along the reservoir rim, can be extensive. More than half the area of the vast, shallow Caniapiscau reservoir, for instance, is in the drawdown zone, subject alternately to drying or to flooding by these artificial tides.

Some drowned trees still stand in the La Grande complex drawdown zones, but many have been broken by the weight of the collars of ice which form around them early in winter. They float on the water. Blown by the wind, they pile up on the reservoir banks.

Even if these banks were not cluttered by dead trees, natural shoreline plants could not grow on them. In summer, when the water level drops in natural lakes or streams, it rises in reservoirs, drowning any plants that do manage to get established. The rims of reservoirs do not, and can not, replace any of the lost wetland habitat; they are broad, lifeless banks of mud, rock, and dead trees.

The builders of the La Grande complex have also left traces in reducing the flow of three major rivers: the Caniapiscau, the Koksoak and, the most drastically reduced, the Eastmain. With its beautiful rapids and cascades, the Eastmain River was a canoeist's joy. It is now, in places, a trickle. Water from the tributaries falling into the truncated section of the Eastmain, downstream from the cut-off dam, erodes its desiccated banks. Its water, in consequence is turbid. Fish, such as the sturgeon, that like clear, deep water are gone now, and so are the muskrat and beaver that once found food and shelter along its shores.

The builders of the La Grande complex have increased the flow in the zones through which water diverted from the Eastmain and from the Caniapiscau passes from the two peripheral reservoirs into those along the La Grande. They have also greatly increased the flow in the La Grande River below the LG-2 reservoir. Averaged over the year, the flow here is double what it was in nature. In mid-winter, when water is being rapidly drawn from the reservoir to generate electricity, the flow is as much as ten times greater than it was here under natural conditions (and it will increase even further when the LG-2A powerhouse is in operation.)[2]

Eroded by this heavy flow, the banks of the La Grande are slipping, slumping and sliding into the river. A number of traditional fishing sites have been ruined, and even the sand bluffs on which the new community of Chisasibi has been built are threatened. (This is ironic, for the people moved here fearing the island on which they formerly lived would be washed away.) Another physical result of the increased flow is that the ice breaks up at the mouth of the La Grande River earlier than it did under natural conditions.

Though the quarries and construction sites, and the dams, dikes, roads and airports, occupy much less area than do the reservoirs and altered rivers, they too constitute traces of human presence in the James Bay region. In the early 1970s, as construction began, contractors worked in an even quicker and dirtier manner than they would have if they had been building in sight of civilization, in the South. They threw roads across spawning sites in lakes, for instance, and after excavating sand and gravel, left tracts of barren land. By 1977, however, the Energy

Corporation had drawn up environmental protection guidelines which were more stringent than the province's, and had placed inspectors, mostly young graduates in ecology or environmental engineering, at every work camp to see that the new rules were respected. Dikes were built around stacks of fuel drums to contain spills. Where convenient, sand and gravel were excavated from sites that would later be flooded. Where this could not be done, bulldozers stockpiled topsoil before removing sand or gravel, and before leaving the excavated pit, they smoothed its slopes and spread the topsoil back again.

Millions of plants — mainly the pioneering, colonizing species, jack pine, willow and alder — have been planted in an effort to reforest zones stripped by construction, as well as to reduce erosion on sections of the banks of desiccated rivers. This has been done, however, in only a fraction of damaged areas, those along the most-used roads and around the most-visited installations. It will take a long time before the scattered plants reseed the barren spaces between them.

John Spence told me that René Lévesque, seeing a dirty plume of sediment spreading into James Bay from the mouth of the Eastmain River, said "This won't do." In conjunction with SOTRAC — Société des travaux de correction du Complexe La Grande (La Grande Remedial Works Corporation), an organization created by the James Bay and Northern Québec Agreement to repair environmental damage affecting Cree hunting, fishing and trapping — the Energy Corporation responded with one of its many technical fixes: it built sills. These minor dams raise the water level, making the dried-up river look like a lake. They allow boats and snowmobiles to use sections of the river. They help create habitat appropriate for some fish, and for the animals that live on the river banks. Muskrat and beaver have returned, according to the Energy Corporation, and slightly more wild waterfowl are nesting along the Eastmain River now than did before it was diverted. And it no longer leaves traces, in the form of sediment plumes, of how it has been changed.

To compensate the Indians for the loss of wildlife habitat, and thus of food (and furs), the Energy Corporation took steps to facilitate fishing in the reservoirs from which, it claimed, more food would come than had come from the land it inundated. It tried to preserve or establish spawning grounds in selected zones of the reservoirs, for instance; it built roads and docks, and it cleared trees. Floating trees are obstacles to travel and to fishing: they snag on nets, hinder boats, clog spawning grounds, block fish from swimming to and from tributaries. One of the steps the Energy Corporation took, therefore, was to clear floating debris from parts of the La Grande-2 and Opinaca reservoirs. It tried, among other things, fishing trees from the reservoirs and burning them in a floating incinerator. This *machine infernale* — as one frustrated cadre called it — was not a success: it cost a lot but achieved little.

To identify those areas where such technical fixes could reduce the impacts on nature and on Natives of what it was building, the Energy Corporation made an ecological inventory, and monitored changes to the ecosystem as construction proceeded. André Dumouchel led the 45 biologists who, in 1973, began gathering such data for the Energy Corporation in the James Bay region. To "the old gang," he told me — the surveyors and construction workers already in the field — his staff "seemed buffoons, counting bugs and animals."[3]

Until 1978, the federal government's environment ministry collaborated with the Energy Corporation and with Hydro-Québec on a major environmental study of the James Bay region. Since then, the Energy Corporation and its parent have continued such work alone. In an ongoing program, technicians sample water and fish, thus monitoring changes in the reservoirs and diversion zones, and the Energy Corporation has hired biologists to carry out numerous studies in the field.

* * *

The only part of the La Grande complex area used by caribou, according to Energy Corporation's wildlife biologists, was in the east, in and around the area which the Caniapiscau reservoir would flood. Here several hundred females returned, year after year, to give birth to their calves. Since caribou move readily, and since only a small fraction of the caribou range would be flooded, the biologists expected that the caribou would readily establish new calving grounds. To verify this expectation, however, the biologists needed to track the caribou movements. Caribou travel hundreds of kilometres every year. They can only be tracked, at considerable expense, from the air. Thus, as the Caniapiscau reservoir was filling, biologists herded caribou into nets in which their antlers became tangled, fastened collars carrying radio transmitters around their necks and released them. Later, flying in helicopters, the biologists located and plotted the caribou movements — and thus verified their expectations.

The Energy Corporation also used radio telemetry and helicopters to find out how beaver responded to the flooding. The rising water forced the beaver to move up into the forest. Here they found little food, and little shelter from the jaws of wolves, lynx, foxes. They were decimated. A few survivors built lodges above the high water marks on the edges of reservoirs, with long tunnels reaching into the water below the low water line, but after one winter, they gave up struggling to survive in such a bizarre environment.

Of all the land flooded by the La Grande complex, that nearest James Bay had the most beaver. In the area to be inundated by the Opinaca reservoir, the Energy Corporation experimented with an expensive rescue operation: it caught a hundred or so live beavers, flew them by helicopter to areas that would not be flooded, and released them. The corporation organized a less extravagant program in the areas to be flooded by the LG-2 and LG-3 reservoirs; here Cree trappers simply harvested all the beavers.

ORT

Most maps of the La Grande Complex show only the upper, diverted portion of the Caniapiscau River; its lower portion, in which flow has been reduced, is considered to be outside the complex — but not beyond range of its impacts. The Energy Corporation, in conjunction with the Inuit, studied the effects of reducing flow in the Caniapiscau on the salmon of the Koksoak, into which the Caniapiscau flows, and hence on the Inuit of Kuujjuaq (formerly Fort Chimo). Members of this community, which is near the mouth of the Koksoak, net, eat, and sell salmon. The base camp for these field studies was an abandoned Hudson's Bay Company trading post known as Fort McKenzie. This cluster of log buildings sits on a natural terrace laced with caribou trails by the Swampy Bay River, near its confluence with the Caniapiscau. The country around is rugged, wild, and beautiful.

At Fort McKenzie I met, among other people, a biologist who spent his days dressed in a dry diving suit and wearing a diver's mask — the outline of which was marked on his face by insect bites and sunburn — crawling up tributaries of the Caniapiscau rock by rock, counting young salmon.

There I joined an archaeological dig. I had to protect myself from the voracious blackflies by sealing my clothing with elastic bands and tape at ankles and wrists, with towels at the neck, and by splashing any remaining patches of exposed skin with bug dope. I spent the day kneeling in a one-meter square pit, scraping the thin soil with a trowel. It would have been exciting to find some of the surprisingly sharp quartzite and jasper arrow heads, skin scrapers, or bone knives that other diggers had found, or some of the circle of stones that held down skins around the circumference of a tepee, or some of the fire-blackened hearth stones. But I found nothing. Unlike the Energy Corporation, the Natives of this land have left hardly a trace of their presence.

In July 1984 I was on the banks of the Caniapiscau in the company of a geomorphologist and many migrating caribou. No one can be sure of the size of the George River herd — some estimate it as more than 600,000 head — but everyone agrees it is the largest in the world. In the 1950s it numbered less than 5,000. Its population has been exploding, and the herd has been expanding its range. Once found mainly around the George River —which flows parallel to and east of the Caniapiscau — the herd now migrates across much of the Quebec-Labrador Peninsula, and some of its members are increasingly found near James Bay. The valley of the Caniapiscau is one of its major migration routes; in late summer the caribou begin heading toward their wintering ground, following the river north and swimming across it from east to west. (These caribou reverse the common pattern, in which animals head south for winter.)

Watching these wild creatures flowing over the hill tops, hatched with ragged trees, and down the wide beaches of the Caniapiscau was a stirring experience. Singly, and in groups of a dozen or so, they sauntered, grazing, resting. The leader of one group settled to the sand, buckling first his front legs, then his rear. His followers did likewise. Their antlers were wide, sweeping, velvet-covered. Liquid brown eyes gazed in my direction, wide with curiosity, I thought, but not fear. When I begin to peel an orange, however, the caribou snorted, rose, and trotted away, stiff-legged, bouncing, their ankle bones clicking like castanets.

Group after group approached the river, hesitated, sniffing for danger. Then one waded in, and the others followed. Heads high out of the water, snorting like dyspeptic gluttons, they swam strongly, clambered out on the far shore, shook themselves, and moved on down the Caniapiscau.

I found a trail of blood on the sand, and followed it into a natural amphitheatre in the dunes. Here the tracks of a caribou and of a wolf — its paw print as big as the palm of my hand — spiraled round each other. There was a caribou calf at the centre of the spiral, still alive, but dying; it had a sucking wound in its lungs, a punctured stomach, an open neck. The highways the caribou follow — like those we drive on — are killing grounds.

A few days before this, I had been at La Grande-4 with members of the Environmental Expert Committee of the Energy Corporation. This consultative committee acts as an umpire: it evaluates measures taken by the Energy Corporation to minimize impacts on the environment, and makes suggestions. Its members include representatives of the Native signatories of the James Bay and Northern Québec Agreement. The first phase of the La Grande complex was almost complete then, in 1984, and the environmental experts were taking a near-final look at its eastern end. In particular, they were looking at the region where, during the winter of 1983-1984, water had spread out, overflowing streams and lakes, drowning swamps and woods, on its way down to the La Grande-4 reservoir after being released from the Caniapiscau reservoir for the first time. Armand Couture, chairman of the committee of experts, explained to me the concern that where this water flowed rapidly it would form frazil ice — the sticky ice that accumulates at the bottom of a rapid — and pile up ice dams. Such dams might have diverted water north over the divide into the Great Whale River basin, to flow down to salt water without generating electricity. Couture was quietly jubilant. No water had been lost that past winter, and the environmental experts, who had crammed into helicopters to look for problems such as banks made unstable by the flow of diverted water, had found none, and anticipated none.

Two taps drain the Caniapiscau reservoir: one, the Brisay control structure, allows water to drain down to the La Grande River; the other, built into the dam that cut off the Caniapiscau, allows the river to be used as a spillway. When I was on the Caniapiscau in July 1984 the tap at Duplanter was closed. The river was shallow, in consequence, and the wide beaches along which the caribou strolled were, in fact, exposed sections of river bed. Downstream, in Kuujjuaq, the Inuit complained that their boats were running aground, and asked that Hydro-Québec let more water flow down the river.

Early in September 1984, after almost three years of filling, the Caniapiscau reservoir was full. Hydro-Québec could not sell all the energy stored in the form of water. Unless some water was spilled, the reservoir would overflow when the autumn rains began, destroying its dikes. To spill large quantities down the La Grande-2 spillway would worsen the damage that pounding water and pebbles had already done to its concrete bed. So Hydro-Québec began spilling its largest reservoir down the Caniapiscau River.

Then it began to rain cats and dogs. Swollen both by the water being spilled from the reservoir, and by run-off from the torrential rains, the Caniapiscau, a particularly flashy river, rose so high that in its lower reaches it washed away an Inuit hunting camp away. The Inuit asked the Energy Corporation to reduce the spilling. It did so on 28 September.

The effect of reducing flow through the Duplanter control structure had not yet been felt at Limestone Falls, 400 kilometres downstream when, probably on 30 September, more than 10,000 caribou approached. Limestone Falls, the last in the series of narrow, steep drops over which the Caniapiscau plunges on its way to the sea, is one of the places where the caribou traditionally cross the river. Pushed from behind, those in front had no choice but to enter the raging, white, tumult of water. The rest followed. Within about four hours, almost all were swept over the falls, smashed on the rocks, and drowned.

The river swept their carcasses downstream and strewed them on its banks like tangled driftwood. Alerted by the number of floating carcasses, a caribou biologist who happened to be in the area flew up the Caniapiscau by helicopter, discovered what had happened, and alerted the world press. The cameras arrived in time to take dramatic photographs of a few survivors, stranded on a barren island above the falls and swathed in mists, and of the thousands of tangled dead.

This drowning looked like an ecological catastrophe, and many people so categorized it, and blamed it on mismanagement by Hydro-Québec.

Adducing hydrological data, the utility and its subsidiary, the Energy Corporation, denied responsibility for the drowning. Most of the water that swept the caribou away was run-off from the torrential rains. If the dam had not existed, the flow at Limestone Falls would have been even heavier, since the amount of water being spilled at the Duplanter control structure early in September was less than what had been observed to flow there at that time of year before the dam was built. The drowning, in the words of a Hydro-Québec spokesman, was "mainly an act of God:" it was He who made the rain fall, and made the caribou stupid.

Why did the caribou cross at such a dangerous spot at such a dangerous time? Did the roar of the rushing water attract the gregarious beasts? Did it sound to them like the noise their kind makes, a blend of snuffling and snorting, of the clatter of heel bones and the rumble of hooves hitting ground? Or were they lulled into a false sense of security by the fact that crossing at Limestone Falls had been safe during the previous few years when, because the Caniapiscau reservoir was being filled, the river had been exceptionally low? I doubt such questions can be answered. They were not addressed in the provincial government's closed enquiry, which exonerated the Energy Corporation.

Could the drowning have been avoided? Yes, if Hydro-Québec had foreseen its possibility, and had reduced the amounts it was spilling from the Caniapiscau reservoir when the unusually heavy rains began. A hydroelectric complex changes a self-regulating watershed into one that must be managed. But though Hydro-Québec has taken over many of nature's responsibilities in this bioregion, it is unwilling to accept them all. And no one concerned with the potential impacts of the hydroelectric project, neither developers nor critics, had paid much attention to caribou which, migrating through territories far from the reservoirs, seemed invulnerable.

In fact, the drowning had little effect on the George River caribou. Hunters kill more of these beasts every year than were drowned, and

biologists estimate that 50,000 could be culled annually without en-
dangering the health of the large and still-growing herd. The drowning, I
think, was a freak accident, and the lesson it teaches is that, no matter
how smart or well-intentioned you are, you cannot predict all the consequences on flora, fauna, and people of changing the physical environment.[4]

* * *

The developers predicted that the impacts of the La Grande complex
would be slight — that the death it would cause would only serve to shift
ecological balance points slightly. Many of their predictions seem, so far,
to be accurate. Individual creatures have died, but species are doing fine.

Consider the birds. Only a small fraction — about four percent — of
the drainage area of the La Grande complex is habitat suitable for nesting
birds, the developers claimed. Most of this habitat is along the James Bay
coast. Here millions of shore birds and waterfowl feed and rest during
their spring and fall migrations, and many stay during the summer to
nest and raise their young. The developers predicted no significant harm
would be done to these birds. They now claim that although flooding and
changes in river flows have destroyed nesting sites, the number of birds
born in the James Bay region has been reduced by less than one percent.
This loss, they argue, is much less than the number of such birds shot
every year by hunters in Quebec and in the Northeast.[5]

Consider the fish. What the developers predicted of the fish was,
again, new equilibria. There would be a decrease in the populations of
species whose preferred habitats would be inundated. Such species include cisco, the fish most eaten in Northern Canada; it spawns near the
shores of lakes on shallow beds of gravel or sand. On the other hand,
there would be an increase in the populations of species such as pike and
whitefish, which prefer the calm, cold water of lakes.[6]

Though it is early, yet, to get a good idea of how fish are faring —
many individual fish are still older than the reservoirs, and it is difficult to
get meaningful measurements from an outdoor laboratory as big as the
La Grande complex — it seems that this prediction, too, was accurate. But
it was irrelevant; what is probably the most severe of all the consequences of flooding at the La Grande complex — the increase in the level of a
poisonous form of mercury in fish, and hence in Crees — was completely
unpredicted.

When Bourassa launched the La Grande complex, scientists knew
that the levels of mercury were high throughout Northern Canada, even
in pristine water bodies. The mercury comes from natural sources, such as
rock, and from distant industries. Not until the late 1970s, while monitoring a recently-filled reservoir in northern Manitoba, did scientists dis-
cover the disturbing fact that flooding in the North rapidly increases the
concentration of poisonous methylmercury in fish.[7] The decay of flooded
soil and plants, they learned, sets off a complicated series of reactions
which result in bacteria converting mercury from its harmless form into
methylmercury. The mercury in a thermometer is harmless, because it can
not be absorbed. Tiny creatures living in water can absorb methylmercury, however, and do so. Such creatures form the base of a food pyramid,
each layer of which feeds on layers below and furnishes food to those
above. As it rises up this pyramid, methylmercury becomes successively
more concentrated. In the tissues of the fish-eating fish, such as pike and
whitefish, that constitute the topmost layer of the aquatic food pyramid
in the James Bay region, methylmercury concentrations are as much as
six time greater than they were before flooding.

In natural lakes of the James Bay region — lakes the Energy Corporation has not touched — the concentration of methylmercury in fish-
eating fish of average size exceeds 0.5 parts per million.[8] In the La
Grande-2 reservoir it can exceed three parts per million, and in the river
downstream, where fish feed on bits of highly contaminated fish

chopped up the turbines, it can be even higher. Methylmercury can irreversibly damage the nervous system and brain. The saying "mad as a hatter" reminds us of the grim consequences of a former occupational exposure to poisonous forms of mercury. Women who ate mercury-contaminated seafood from industrially-polluted Minamata Bay in Japan gave birth to severely damaged children. The Canadian government prohibits the sale for human consumption of fish containing more than 0.5 parts per million. For Native peoples, who tend to eat more than the quantity of fish assumed in calculating this limit, the threshold of safety is probably 0.2 parts per million.

Because the La Grande reservoirs are like bodies of water into which a nasty industrial chemical has been spilled, it is unsafe for the Crees of Chisasibi — especially for the more vulnerable members of the community, elders, children, and women of child-bearing age — to eat with regularity some kinds of fish caught in the reservoir and in the river downstream. This is a serious loss: fish accounted for a quarter of all the food the Crees used to harvest.[9]

There is controversy as to the level of mercury in a human that can be considered safe. Many Crees have concentrations that exceed what most authorities consider to be maximum acceptable levels. The proportion of a sample of Chisasibi Crees with unacceptable levels rose from about a third in 1977 to two-thirds in 1984. Some Crees show signs of neurological damage such as numbness of limbs and loss of peripheral vision; this, however, does not constitute clear evidence of mercury poisoning, since other things, including alcohol, can cause these symptoms.

Public health authorities considered banning the fishery outright. Alan Penn, one of the Crees' environmental advisers, has pointed out that doing so would probably have an economic and social impact worse than mercury poisoning. Fishing, and sharing the catch, help not only feed but also bind the Cree communities.

Scientists agree that mercury concentrations will eventually diminish to natural background levels as reservoirs age, but the polluting process is too recently discovered and too new for the public to have much confidence in Hydro-Québec's prediction that this will happen in 20 to 30 years. Meanwhile, Hydro-Québec has responded to the mercury problem with money. In 1986 the utility and the Crees signed the Mercury Agreement, under which $18.5-million is being spent on research and on information programs to modify the fishery by informing the Crees on such things as where, when, and for what species it is unsafe to fish. Thanks to such information programs, levels of mercury in the Crees are dropping.

* * *

What has been learned from the great outdoor laboratory of the La Grande complex? Is the modified environment "just as satisfactory as the original natural system," as the Federal Provincial Task Force suggested it would be?

"Our experience has shown that...talk about the extreme fragility of the arctic ecosystem is a myth," says Gaëtan Hayeur, director of natural resources and animal habitat at Hydro-Québec. "Every ecosystem, north and south, has an equilibrium, and what has occurred and will occur is the creation of a new equilibrium in the James Bay territory."[10] Hydro-Québec argues that "not only are [northern ecosystems] robust, but the resources that live here are highly adaptable."[11] Utility spokesmen go on to claim that they have created new beauty, and that the negative impacts of their hydroelectric development are acceptably small. They congratulate themselves on being model corporate citizens; no project of this magnitude, they claim, has ever been built with so much respect and care for the environment. During the decade 1974-1984, the Energy Corporation spent $250-million (about 1.5 percent of the reported total cost of building phase one of the La Grande complex) on environmental studies — the James Bay region is now one of the most intensively studied in the world, they claim — on protection, and on mitigation of the project's adverse effects, especially those harmful to the Crees.[12]

To answer the question about the impacts of the La Grande complex objectively is, for a number of reasons, difficult and perhaps impossible. Ecosystems respond slowly to change. We cannot expect to see all the project's impacts before the end of the century. No comprehensive and independent audit of the impacts has been carried out. As an ecological experiment, the La Grande complex was botched. To assess the impacts of changes to the environment scientists compare data on the changed ecosystem to data on the original, undisturbed ecosystem, but virtually no data were gathered on the fauna and flora of the James Bay region before the bulldozers arrived.

The only assessments that have been made are subjective ones; as the phrase "acceptably small" hints, these assessments are determined by the interests and values of whoever is accepting —or decrying — the impacts. What is acceptable to the Hydro-Québec technocrats who make a living from the La Grande complex is not acceptable to Crees living with it. The project has caused terrible damage, the Crees say: there are fewer and fewer geese and ducks each year; the climate is changing; animals are confused because their migration routes have been disrupted; the La Grande River is dead.

Just as it is in the interests of the developers to minimize the environmental impacts, so it is in the interests of the Crees, who see further plans for further impoundments as threats to their survival as distinct cultural communities, and who are bitterly fighting against them, to exaggerate the environmental impacts. But I suspect that, as well as political expediency, what generates these differences in interpretation are fundamental differences in outlook between those who see the land as something to be used or studied, and those who see it as a community to which they belong and for which they feel love and even reverence. In the Crees' judgement, building the James Bay project is a mortal sin.[13]

I have asked environmental experts who represent Native groups to summarize their views on the project's environmental impacts. Peter Jacobs, who represents the Inuit, told me that "Hydro-Québec is a corporation of very bright engineers with...a great deal of money and an honest desire to deal with environmental issues...In order for three million people in Montreal to have electricity you do have to modify the environment, and the lives of the people who use it. But you can modify it so that they can continue to use it in the traditional way — and so that they too can benefit from the dollars and energy."[14]

Alan Penn, an advisor to the Crees, has criticized the Energy Corporation's environmental monitoring on a number of counts: for instance, he complains that it was designed "not to focus on problems, but to provide general reassurance;" and that "the opportunity to acquire ecologically-relevant information for project planning has been largely missed."[15]

"We have lost major wilderness rivers," he told me. "The La Grande, the Caniapiscau headwater, the Eastmain. The James Bay project has transformed a whole landscape, essentially 10,000 square kilometres, substituting an aquatic for a terrestrial environment. By what criteria is this good or bad? What would amount to a significant impact?" By Penn's scientific criteria there has been "comparatively little disruption," and the impact of the hydroelectric project is "of only transient ecological significance." This view, he added, is heretical to the Crees.[16]

The Energy Corporation's *raison d'être* is not to minimize impacts on the environment, but to maximize the use of it. The corporation did not know what effect it was going to have on the ecosystem. As it turns out, the impacts of flooding the La Grande watershed were not catastrophic. Unlike, say, the ploughing of the Prairies or the burning of the Amazon rain forest, the flooding of the taiga does not seem to be unraveling ecological webs. This is not because of the skills or concern of the developers, I believe, but because of nature, which considers the La Grande complex a venial sin.

NOTES

1. Alain Soucy, "Environmental Planning for a Hydroelectric Project: The La Grande Complex in the James Bay Territory," *International Workshop on Environmental Planning for Large Scale Development Projects*, Whistler, British Columbia (October, 1983). Cited in Rosenthal, *Long-Term Threats to Canada's James Bay*.
2. The LG-2A powerhouse, by adding generators, will enable more power to be generated to meet peak demand. Generating more power means draining the LG-2 reservoir more rapidly.
3. André Dumouchel, interview with author, Montreal, 19 July 1984.
4. For information on the caribou drowning see Lawrence Jackson, "World's largest caribou herd mired in Quebec-Labrador boundary dispute," *Canadian Geographic* (June-July, 1985): 25-33; Québec, *Noyade des caribous sur la rivière Caniapiscau des 28 et 29 Septembre 1984. Rapport du SAGMAI (Secrétariat des activités gouvernementales en milieu amérindien et inuit)* (May 1985); Ted Williams, "Who Killed 10,000 Caribou?" *Audubon Magazine* (March 1985): 12-17.
5. *Le Devoir* (Montreal), 22 February 1990.
6. Cisco is also known as lake herring; in French, as *cisco de lac*; and scientifically, as *Coregonus artedi*. Whitefish is known in French as *grande corégone*, and scientifically as *Coregonus clupeaformis*.
7. The reservoir in question was formed by flooding Southern Indian Lake, and served to divert a portion of the Churchill River into the Nelson River. Both rivers flow into the western side of Hudson Bay. See Hecky, "Methylmercury contamination in northern Canada." See also Charles Dumont, "La mercure à la Baie James," Quatrième conférence, Les Conférences Hydro-Québec: Environnement et Santé, 11 October 1988.
8. Parts per million and milligrams per kilogram are equivalent ways of expressing concentrations.
9. Fikret Berkes, "The Intrinsic Difficulty of Predicting Impacts."
10. Cited by Picard, "James Bay," 17 April 1991.
11. Hydro-Québec. *The Grande Baleine Project. A Project We Can't Do Without* (Hydro-Québec, 1990).

12. Hydro-Québec and the Environment. *Hydro-Québec Development Plan 1989-1991 — Horizon 1998.*
13. See, for instance, Billy Diamond, "Villages of the Dammed."
14. Peter Jacobs, interview with author, Montreal, 20 July 1984.
15. Gorrie, "The James Bay Project," 25; National Energy Board, Hearing Orders No EH-3-89 and AO-1-EH-3-89, Hydro-Québec Applications to Export Electricity to the New York Power Authority and Vermont Joint Owners, Panel No 4 of the Grand Council of the Crees (of Québec), Environmental and Social Aspects, Testimony of Alan Penn, Submitted on February 14, 1990.
16. Alan Penn, interview with the author, Montreal, 2 May 1983.

CHAPTER 7

Changing Native Society

It was early spring in the Cree village of Mistissini. The ground was snow-covered, and the cold wind smelt of wood smoke. Down on the frozen lake, the largest in Quebec, bush planes were taking-off and landing. With stacks of supplies — flour, saws, rifles, decoys — hunters and their families were heading for the bush. Their faces looked like weathered leather, and I was reminded of ethnographer Frank Speck's words: "The Indians of the north have the eyes and mouths of silent men. Their bearing is that of self-centred non-dependent soldiers of chance. Devoid of flippancy, making no exterior exhibition, they do not invite approach."[1]

I was a stranger in the world of the Crees. I wanted to find out how the hydroelectric project which has intruded into their world, flooding parts of the land and bringing with it a flood of influences from the outside, has changed it.

In the new band offices, the chief of the Mistissini band, Matthew Coon-Come, who at the age of 24 became the youngest Cree ever to be elected chief of a band, told me his people did not want more whites visiting. After the James Bay and Northern Québec Agreement was signed, Moonies, kitchenware salesmen, King Fu instructors, dope dealers, social scientists, journalists and others had flocked to Mistissini, looking for business in the most accessible of the Cree communities. Lying just north of the height of land dividing the Saint Lawrence drainage basin from that of James Bay, Mistissini was the only Cree village in Quebec connected by road to the outside world before the La Grande complex was built. "Only where we see that we can benefit directly, we'll agree to answer questions," Coon-Come told me. I was not to be surprised if the police questioned me, for at this time of year many people were going into the bush, leaving their children behind, and this led to alcohol and drug abuse. If I wanted to learn about the social impacts of the James Bay project, I should read what others had written.

The James Bay project has disrupted the lives of Native peoples by physically changing their communities and the forests, rivers and lakes they use, and indirectly, by triggering political rearrangements between Native and non-Native society. The direct disruption varies from place to place. Chisasibi has suffered the greatest range and the most severe of the physical impacts of the James Bay hydroelectric project.

Its people lost more of their hunting and trapping lands than did any other Cree community: six of the 40 traplines on which they hunted and trapped were inundated, and many others were partly flooded. They have lost the use of the lower section of La Grande River. The heavy and fluctuating flow has destroyed habitat needed by small game. The Chisasibi fishery is the one most contaminated with methylmercury. Formerly isolated — literally — on their island, the people and their houses, school, and chapel, were relocated to a new site on shore. There was a sudden influx of money during the construction boom, as the new town was built. It is connected by road to the La Grande-2 construction site. Though the authorities in both communities tried to limit contact, LG-2 has become a conveniently close source of alcohol and drugs. The increased flow in the La Grande River has created transportation problems for the people living at its mouth. The river ice now breaks up earlier than it used to, before the hydroelectric project was built, and, like that of the ice that forms along the coast, its behaviour is unpredictable. From Chisasibi, on the south shore of the river, hunters can no longer safely cross the river ice in spring.

Other communities, too, have felt some of these kinds of impacts. The Natives whose villages are at the mouths of rivers which have been diverted are bothered by the consequences of reduced flow. The ice on the Eastmain River, for instance, breaks up later than it used to, and at goose break time, the people in the village of Eastmain can neither use canoes nor snowmobiles to cross the estuary in safety to get to their goose camps up the coast. Nor can they drink the water from their now-turbid river; their drinking water has to come from a clean source, and be delivered to their homes by truck. Algae slimes fishing nets now in the estuaries of both the Eastmain and the Koksoak Rivers.

Technical fixes can mitigate some of these changes. There is now a bridge across the La Grande at the LG-1 dam site, for instance, and the Energy Corporation has provided helicopters to ferry trappers across unsafe estuaries. And some of the physical changes brought by the hydroelectric project, the developers say, are beneficial — the reservoirs and roads, for instance, give the Crees easier access to hunting lands — and compensate the Natives for lost land.

The Crees do travel on the reservoirs, by boat in summer and by snowmobile in winter. They also use roads, which are the instruments of some of the biggest social impacts of the La Grande complex. The road network includes not only the north-south and east-west axes spanning the entire complex, but also many smaller roads leading to dikes. It once took weeks to paddle and portage from the mouth of the La Grande to the LG-4 region, in the interior of the Quebec-Labrador Peninsula. Now the Crees of Chisasibi can drive there in their trucks in about six hours; some go farther, to the eastern reaches of the James Bay territory, to hunt caribou. As well, now that trucks can supply villages which once could only be reached slowly by train and barge, or expensively by aircraft, the Natives can get cheaper goods and services from the South.

Improved access brings new problems as well as benefits. Some Crees, for instance, have been trapping on areas along roads without the permission of the tallymen, the traditional Native stewards of the land. Bands squabble with other bands over control of territory. Hunters and loggers from the south are moving north up the roads, too, competing with the Crees for use of the southern parts of the James Bay region. Drugs and alcohol move up the roads too.

When Walter Hughboy, chief of the Wemindji band, first flew over the reservoirs of the James Bay project, he felt that something "special and deep had been subtracted from him," that he had "lost his innocence" and was "no longer what he was before."[2] From many similar emotional reports by Crees, we begin to comprehend how a people who see nature as sacred and who have no written history feel about the drowning of hunting grounds, the desiccating and rerouting of rivers, the loss of the campsites, grave sites, and other places imbued with memories, the poisoning of fish, and all the other ramifications of the changes in the James Bay region.

Crees talk with respect about how experienced hunters, by reading subtle signs in nature, can predict such things as when the river ice is safe for travel, when the spring thaw will come, how good the summer fishing will be. But by making the flow regime artificial, the hydroelectric project make these skills obsolete.

Similarly, though mercury pollution in the La Grande reservoirs has not, as far as I know, poisoned anyone directly, it has poisoned the efforts of the Crees to hang on to their traditional culture. By forcing them to recognize a health hazard in what looks like fat and nourishing bush food, it has eroded their confidence in their resources, and hence in the relevance of maintaining the traditional skills for harvesting these resources.

They do not see the hydroelectric project, therefore, as a set of inconveniences, of which some are balanced by benefits, but as a nullifying intrusion, as an assault on their culture.

* * *

With its clusters of wood-clad houses, Chisasibi would resemble a new ski resort if it did not also have the outdoor furnishings of a Native village: snowmobiles; drying caribou and beaver skins; sea-going canoes; fuel drums; tepees for smoking meat and fish, and for putting up visitors. Chisasibi's spatial arrangement, into clusters, embodies the division of the community into three factions — inlanders, south coasters, and north coasters — each distinguished by the areas in which it traditionally hunted and, now, by the cluster of homes in which it has chosen to live. The community centre, a building with a teepee-like tower, houses a hotel, offices and shops. When I was there, there were empty spaces where shops had failed, or never started. Cans, chip bags and other garbage swirled underfoot. The air smelled greasy with frying food, and outdoors there was a whiff of sewage.

There are sensible and decent people in Chisasibi, but it is easy here, maybe easier than anywhere else in northern Quebec, to find illustrations or hear stories of the confusion that rapid change creates, and of social decay. In a bush camp, Crees will stoke up the fire and leave the door flap open so air can circulate. Crees in their new homes in Chisasibi turned the electric heaters up full-blast, while leaving doors and windows open. The result, of course, was high electricity bills. Rather than sharing the geese they shoot, some young Crees now sell them, a disturb-ing innovation for their elders. Hundreds of teenagers board in Chisasibi while finishing high school. With no parents to supervise them, some break windows in their school and engage in other acts of vandalism. Some people spend hundreds of dollars a week on booze; others, the most self-destructive, sniff glue or gasoline. Drunk men beat their wives and children. In an attempt to control the alcohol problem there is now a check-point at which vehicles are searched on the road into Chisasibi. The incidence of teenage pregnancies and sexually transmitted diseases is high. The death rate among adolescents and young adults has increased sharply due to accidents, homicides, and suicides, most related to alcohol abuse.

One of the sad ironies of life in northern Quebec is that so many health problems are self-inflicted. The Native peoples here were among the poorest of Canada's poor. They now enjoy decent sanitation and health care facilities, and the incidence of the classic illnesses of poverty such as tuberculosis has been greatly reduced. But the prevalence of emotional problems, and of diseases related to poor diet, has increased. Many kids have rotten teeth. Diabetes, of which there were no cases among the Crees until the 1980s, and heart disease, which was very rare, are becoming common, and so too is obesity, as any visitor to Chisasibi can attest. Traditionally, the Crees, like all northern hunting peoples, ate a lot of fat. In the past, when many hungry days could elapse between meals, their ability to store this fat in their bodies helped them survive, and tramping and paddling kept them in superb physical condition. Many Natives now lead sedentary lives — they have trucks, outboard motors, skidoos. They eat less fish than before, for fear of mercury poison-ing, and more store-bought foods — and those rich in fat, sugar, and carbohydrates, including junk food and candy, are popular.

"We want the best of both worlds, the traditional and the modern," James Bobbish, former chief of Chisasibi, told me, "but what we experience is the worst of both worlds."[3] It would be unfair to blame this entirely on the James Bay project. In response to the ideas, images, and values of the dominant world culture disseminated by television, music, and many other means, cultures everywhere are changing. You do not have to have your land flooded or stolen to be dispossessed of your identity, and many Native communities in North America, like Chisasibi, are slowly imploding, a symptom, some say, of the loss of cultural identity.

Social stress is not something that can easily be measured or compared, or for which clear causes can be found. The impression I have formed is that Chisasibi shows the most severe signs of social stress of all the Native communities in northern Quebec, and that this is connected to the fact that it is the community most severely affected by the hydroelectric project. A visit to Wemindji, the Cree community to the south of Chisasibi, reinforced this impression. Wemindji sits on a protected bay, where the Mataqua flows into James Bay. The hydroelectric project did not touch this river, but it did touch the community. The Opinaca reservoir and diversion zone flooded, in whole or in part, 12 of Wemindji's 35 traplines. With money received in compensation for this loss, Wemindji has built sewage lines, a water supply, houses, and an arena. Unlike Chisasibi, however, Wemindji has not experienced any sudden major influx of non-Natives, or boom period of high employment. With only about 750 people it is smaller than Chisasibi, and more cohesive. What is probably most significant of all in damping the impacts on it is that it is more isolated; it is still only accessible by winter road, by sea, or by air.

Even to a casual visitor, Wemindji is a more traditional place than Chisasibi, and a more welcoming one. What I remember of it is the old men playing checkers on homemade boards under the trees, and the kids playing on the sandy beach and splashing in the river.

*　*　*

In the bad old days, the dominant society cleared Natives from the land it wanted to develop with guns and germs. Today, it integrates Natives into its rational, bureaucratic order and gives them money. To clear the way for the *projet du siècle* (project of the century), the developers conceded power and money to the Natives according to complex arrangements spelled out in the 500 pages of the James Bay and Northern Québec Agreement, and in the 250 supplementary pages of its amendments and related agreements. These political rearrangements have triggered a Quiet Revolution among the Natives in northern Quebec which resembles that of the 1960s among the Québécois in southern Quebec — a period marked by rapid modernization, the creation of nation-building bureaucracies, national affirmation, and the politics of victimization.

The agreements created a plethora of new bodies, boards, committees, councils and other bureaucratic entities — enough to run a province, some say — and all run by Native peoples or at least with their participation. These entities include the Grand Council of Crees (of Québec) and the Cree Regional Authority, the political and administrative bodies in the Cree homeland; and, north of the 55th parallel, in the Inuit homeland, their counterparts, the Makivik Society and the Kativik Regional Administration. These regional government bodies invest the more than $500-million in compensation that the Natives have or will receive under the agreements, forming heritage funds which — it was hoped — would make the Natives economically self-reliant. Using interest income and some of their capital as seed money, these regional bodies have launched service enterprises such as Cree Construction Company, and two airlines, Air Creebec and Air Inuit. (Though the goal of these enterprises is to make money, they do not necessarily do so. Air Creebec, for instance, the pride of the Crees, has lost millions.)

As well, the Native bureaucracy includes organizations such as the Cree School Board, the Cree Board of Health, and the Cree Housing Society. Quebec and Ottawa promised to transfer money to these organizations to build and run new schools, hospitals, houses, water supply and sewage systems, and other community facilities. Though these organizations are ultimately under the jurisdiction of ministries of the Quebec government, Natives living in the James Bay region, not distant, paternalistic non-Native bureaucrats, now exercise local control over the services delivered to their communities. Both Crees and Inuit have decided to launch programs to build new houses and infrastructure in their villages. The Crees have decided that the language of instruction during the first three years of school should be Cree, and that the spring goose break should be a school holiday.

The interest earned on the $500-million or so in compensation money pays for only about a tenth of what it takes to run the economy of the James Bay region. The rest comes in the form of payments from government for services — payments which, between 1975 and 1990, amount, approximately, to another $500-million. The Native economy is heavily subsidized.

To a tourist from the South who has read about how things were in northern Quebec, the resulting improvements in the material conditions of life are striking. The Crees and Inuit live in new houses, hooked up to running water and sewers. They have new dispensaries, nursing stations or hospitals, and schools, hockey arenas, and airstrips. They enjoy the services of a typical North American suburb — something which few other Native communities do. Even the three dissident Inuit villages have received schools and houses, though less than those communities that voted for the agreement.

Because of such improvements, the Native population is increasing rapidly. Throughout the Americas, aboriginal peoples were decimated by contact with Europeans, who carried infectious diseases to which the Natives had no resistance. By the 1930s the Cree population, cruelly checked by both famine and disease, reached a nadir of around 1,500. It began to grow, slowly, after World War Two. Since 1970, the infant mortality rate, which was three times higher than Quebec's, has dropped by more than half, life expectancy has increased, and the population has doubled. There are now about 12,000 Crees in Quebec — about as many as when their ancestors first met Europeans. Youth predominate; more than 65 percent of the Crees are under 25 years old.

The average income of James Bay Cree households, according to the 1986 census, is around $34,000, slightly more than the average for Quebec, and more than twice that in Cree communities on the Ontario side of James Bay. The cost of living in the North is high — a chicken in Chisasibi costs at least $20 — and families are relatively large. Counterbalancing this is the fact that Native peoples do not pay taxes. As a result, real incomes in northern Quebec are at comfortable levels, and Native peoples here can afford stereos, microwaves, pick-up trucks, snowmobiles, high-powered rifles with telescopic sights, and televisions.

The Hunters and Trappers Income Security Program, the only provision of the James Bay and Northern Québec Agreement which pays money directly to individuals, and a key tool by which the Crees hoped to keep their hunting culture alive, now supports about one-third of all the Crees. This program pays hunters or trappers some $11,000 a year — the amount varies with, among other factors, time spent in the bush. Encouraged by this program, many Crees are now hunting for longer periods than in the early 1970s, and catching more meat. They now bring two-way radios, which are continually monitored in their villages, generators, washing machines, chain saws, snowmobiles, disposable diapers, and other products of industrial society into the bush — whatever will make life outdoors in the sub-Arctic less dangerous, grim, and grueling. Despite the gadgets, they are keeping alive the customs, knowledge, and attitudes that comprise their hunting culture and the touchstone of their identity. "We are the hunting people," they say.

One of the things that hunting and trapping signify to the Crees is self-reliance. "If you can subsist in the bush," a Cree told me, "you are never dependent on a job, you can never be fired." But hunting and trapping never provided much beyond the bare necessities of life, and now the cost of getting 15 beaver pelts, about the average annual harvest of a Cree trapper, is a good deal more than what those pelts fetch when sold. The mechanized aids a trapper uses are costly, and the bottom has fallen out of the fur market, in part because the anti-fur lobby has persuaded many in the general public that trapping is cruel. Neither the fur nor the meat the Crees bring home can pay for the gear, houses, health care and other things they consume. Hunting and trapping are no longer economically viable, and like rice farmers in Japan and dairy farmers in Ireland, Cree hunters live on subsidies.

There is, in Native society, a growing gulf between the elders, who remember the past and life in the bush and the world of dreams and spirits, and the youth in their leather jackets and Nike sneakers and their rock video dreams. Hunters are a declining proportion of the total Cree population. Many youth, especially those who have been schooled, have become too assimilated to non-Native culture to be attracted to the strenuous hunting life, and to have acquired the necessary skills; and even if more people wanted to hunt, they could not, for the land can not sustain a harvest of wildlife greater than the current one. Not many youth have enough education to get fulfilling jobs in the weighty Native bureaucracy, which provides most of the permanent jobs in northern Quebec. There are, as yet, as far as I know, no Native doctors or engineers or pilots or flight attendants, and few Native teachers or nurses.

Some people work for the Cree Construction Company which, among other things, maintains roads and builds construction camps for Hydro-Québec, but the number of such jobs has dropped since the construction boom, when the Crees were building new houses and facilities for their communities. Native wealth-producing enterprises are rare. There is a silver fox fur ranch in Wemindji, and a canoe factory in Waskaganish, a joint venture between the band and the Canadian subsidiary of the Japanese Yamaha Corporation. Other than these businesses, which employ a handful of people, there is little else. "There is a good deal of truth in the criticism that Indians are lazy and dependent," one Cree told me, "but it is not by their choice. The Crees like to work, to achieve things with their hands. But now there are so few things to work at."

The biggest long-term problem the Natives of northern Quebec face is that of finding occupations for their ever increasing number of young people, more than half of whom, now, are unemployed.

Nowhere in the sub-Arctic, it seems to me, is a self-sufficient regional economy, one that actually creates wealth and pays its own way, likely to develop. This is in part because of tradition. Cultures that are indifferent to the logic of acquisition, and to the discipline of the clock and the boss, produce few entrepreneurs. Traders who raised the prices paid for furs in the last century, hoping this would entice the Indians to trap more, were perplexed, for it had the opposite effect: the more the Indians got for their furs, the sooner they met their needs, and so they trapped less. Traditionally, Natives measure time not by clock and calendar, but by seasons and animal movements, and they followed not the orders of another person, but the prompting of their own dreams and inclinations.

Even if there were Native entrepreneurs, how could they produce wealth in the sub-Arctic? The biological resources are poor. Markets and supplies are far away. Almost anything that can be done or grown there can be done or grown more cheaply in the south. The list of possible ways to produce wealth in the James Bay region, then, is a short one: it includes commercially harvesting caribou, running tours for hunters and adventurers, logging and other forestry operations in the southern parts of the region, mining, and, of course, hydroelectric projects. And in signing the Natives James Bay and Northern Québec Agreement, the Natives explicitly renounced the claim they might have made, based on the concept of aboriginal rights, to ownership of the more economically valuable of these resources, and in particular, to ownership of water rights.

The Natives of northern Quebec face a terrible dilemma. They cannot live where they do, and as they do, without subsidies. Yet to depend on subsidies is a dead end, as Harry Tulugak, a leader of the dissident Inuit, has explained; for if all you do is claim rights and money, if all you know about is getting and spending money, not about earning it, then you lose your sense of responsibility.

* * *

The key to advancement in Native communities now is politics. The brightest and the best-educated of the Natives of northern Quebec — those who bridge the gaps not only between elders and youth within their communities, but also between the culture of the Crees and that of the non-Native world; those who are at ease arguing with ministers and deputy-ministers; hiring money managers, tax lawyers, consultant energy analysts, and Madison Avenue public relations firms; flying from meeting to exhausting meeting, articulating their peoples' discontents to the world — hold the few prestigious, well-paying jobs that exist in the James Bay region. Wits have wondered whether there are enough Natives in the James Bay region to attend all the meetings the complex new political order requires. There are; they constitute one of the most remarkable impacts of the agreements, and thus, indirectly of the hydroelectric project: the creation of a politically-sophisticated Native elite.

Once, on the desk of Walter Hughboy, chief of Wemindji, I saw an enormous stack of documents held down by a rifle — apt symbols, I thought of the two cultural modes, hunter and bureaucrat, in which Native leaders function. There is continuity between these modes; getting power and money in a hostile environment calls for shrewdness and self-reliance just as does harvesting furs and meat. But there is a rupture too; in order to preserve their traditional hunting culture, Native leaders have had to abandon it, to become what they call "briefcase Indians."

Despite the fact that the contractual provisions of the James Bay and Northern Québec Agreement and its related agreements have been incorporated into both federal and provincial laws, and embedded in the Canadian constitution, some of the promises made in these agreements have not been honoured. Both Crees and Inuit have been dragging the governments before the courts, trying to force them to provide promised money for, among other things, education, health, infrastructure, and for houses — of which the Natives, with their expanding population, are chronically short. At the beginning of the 1980s, for instance, an epidemic of gastroenteritis, a disease associated with poor sanitation and the lack of running water, killed eight children and hospitalized 80. The Crees mainly blamed Quebec, which had not yet funded promised sanitation facilities. A federal review of the problems in implementing the Agreement, organized in response to the Natives' bitter complaints, accused government bureaucrats of honouring the Agreement only in the narrowest sense, and of taking no pains to make it work. In 1983, the federal government decided to give $60-million more to the Crees.

The main problem with implementing the Agreement, from the governments' point of view, is that in signing it they promised to deliver services the costs of which were not made explicit and which have turned out to be higher than predicted. (Between 1975 and the year 2000 the number of beneficiaries of the Agreement will have trebled, and the costs, per person, of providing services such as health care to distant and widely scattered communities are huge.) The Crees "got a slightly better deal than they expected," Alan Penn told me. "They got a formidable amount of money."[4]

The Native leaders complain that they have not been able to exercise any significant control over decisions affecting their region. The mechanisms, such as joint committees, which were to give them power to participate actively in economic development in their land — not just as beneficiaries, but as controllers — do not work. For instance, the Crees have not been able to stop the loggers who, with Quebec's permission, are now clear-cutting most of the harvestable timber in the southern portion of the Cree homeland (including lands which Hydro-Québec hopes to flood in the Nottaway-Broadback-Rupert complex).

"The shock is going to be brutal," a staff anthropologist for the James Bay Development Corporation said during the Malouf hearings. "Perhaps it is the only way to make a culture react, and then really begin to participate, to take its own development in hand." The Agreements which were hailed as a mechanism by which the Natives would become virtually self-governing and self-reliant have not brought about either end. They have not even provided the social peace the developers hoped for. The relationship between Natives and governments in northern Quebec is peevish. Just to arrange the date and agenda of a meeting can take months of negotiation.

The developers claim that the Crees exaggerate the social as well as the ecological impacts of the hydroelectric project. The developers acknowledge that they might have made some better choices of technical fixes; rather than building access ramps to the La Grande complex reservoirs, for instance, they should have built snowmobile trails so Crees could set up fishing camps on distant lakes. But the developers insist that though the Natives have had to adjust, moving to fresh lakes and fresh hunting grounds, even with the La Grande complex built they can continue to live off the land, and some do. The developers agree that Native lives have been changed, but claim that this was bound to happen, and that the Natives have been generously compensated for their inconvenience. "Why do the Natives never say anything positive," Jacques Guevremont has asked. "Why do they never talk about the benefits they have received?"

They do not do so because they feel so much resentment. They resent the pressure on them to sign the Agreements from which these benefits flow, pressure exerted by the massive scale and momentum of the James

Bay project. They resent the physical changes to their land and lives caused by its intrusion. They resent their growing dependence on the State. They resent all the changes that have swept through their communities in the past two decades, and they blame these changes on the developers. But the Cree leaders have more to do than resent the past; they have new problems.

A few years ago, hunters from the community of Great Whale River, who hardly ever encountered strangers, Native or non-Native, began seeing helicopters zooming overhead, landing pads hacked out of the scrawny forest, surveyors' ribbons and stakes. Surveyors, hydrologists, and geologists were exploring and mapping the routes for more roads and power lines, the sites for more construction camps, the pits from which more rock will be excavated and dumped into more rapids, the ground on which more dams will stand, and the land which more reservoirs will inundate. They were starting work on the Great Whale hydroelectric project, the first of the James Bay II megaprojects. The Cree leaders are focusing their formidable political skills on stopping it.

NOTES

1. Speck, *Nascapi*, 245.
2. Wittenborn, *James Bay Project*, 109.
3. James Bobbish, interview with author, Chisasibi, 30 July 1984.
4. Alan Penn, interview with the author, Montreal, 3 June 1983.

PART THREE

James Bay II

CHAPTER 8

Proponents

In 1983, Robert Bourassa won back his former job as leader of the Quebec Liberal Party, because, as journalist Graham Fraser put it, "he wanted it more than anyone else — and he out-worked, out-hustled, out-campaigned, and out-toughed anyone who might have taken it from him."[1] During the summer of 1985, Bourassa campaigned for the coming provincial elections, criss-crossing the province in a chartered aircraft named *L'Énergie du Nord*. This is also the title of the book he released that summer. In that book — its English version is called *Power from the North* — and in the election campaign, Bourassa reiterated and amplified his proposal to harness the rivers of the Quebec-Labrador Peninsula.

The dams he wanted to build, as soon as possible, would generate 12,000 megawatts for export to the northeastern United States, and they would attract dynamic new industries to Quebec. All heavy consumers of electricity, these new industries would need the power when the export contracts expired. The more electricity Quebec generated, he promised, the more prosperous a place it would become, with jobs for all. "First things first," he told me during the 1985 campaign. "If you don't have jobs you have deficits, you have despair, you have discouragement, and you have division. You have to be able to provide jobs to those who are ready to work. Otherwise...they will be unhappy."[2]

"Quebec is a vast hydroelectric plant in the bud," he wrote, "and every day, millions of potential kilowatthours flow downhill and out to sea. What a waste!"[3] Not only the energy of free-flowing rivers was being wasted, according to Bourassa, but also their water. He promoted the GRAND (for Great Recycling and Northern Development) Canal scheme, in which some 160 kilometres of dikes would be built across James Bay to turn it into a fresh water reservoir the size of Lake Superior. The water would be pumped over the height of land to drain down into the Great Lakes and, from there, through many connecting waterways and canals, to the Canadian Prairies and to the American Midwest and Southwest. The GRAND Canal scheme would turn the continent's water systems into an interconnected grid to carry water to its parched and distant regions from James Bay.

The Parti Québécois was in power, but in disarray. René Lévesque had resigned as leader after refusing, for reasons of political expediency, to fight another election on the issue of independence. Bourassa castigated the Parti Québécois for not pushing firm sales of electricity, and for not pushing ahead with construction of the James Bay project. In December 1985, when the first phase of this project was completed with the commissioning of the La Grande-4 powerhouse, the Liberals roundly defeated the Parti Québécois. "La Grande has once again become the almost exclusive province of the beaver, caribou, and mink," Bourassa wrote "and the austere beauty of the north is undisturbed except for the rushing of the river's waters. At least for now." But now the man whose only unwavering political commitment has been to hydroelectric development, and whose political career has been inextricably entwined with the James Bay project — "*La Baie James*," he has regally declared, "*c'est Bourassa*" (James Bay is Bourassa) — was once again Premier of Quebec.

Hydro-Québec's plans, though considerably more modest than Bourassa's, are ambitious enough. To meet Quebec's needs 25 years hence, the utility expects it will have harnessed all of the 19,000 or so megawatts that could be harnessed from Quebec's rivers for a cost less than that of alternative sources of energy. It has ranked future hydroelectric projects in order of cost, and established a schedule for building these projects, starting with the least expensive. It revises this schedule every year, as its estimates of demand change. The main difference between Hydro-Québec's plans and Bourassa's is that Hydro-Québec is reluctant to develop its rivers as rapidly as Bourassa would like.

Because, in part, of the contracts negotiated by Jacques Guevremont and his team of salesmen, Hydro-Québec has been selling its surpluses. American utilities have been saving money by replacing some of the output of their coal-fired and oil-fired power stations with cheap electricity from Quebec. Even before Bourassa returned to power, Hydro-Québec moved into the second stage of its export development plan. It saw a profitable opportunity in selling firm electricity to the northeast states, which could, by buying this electricity, postpone having to build new nuclear-powered or coal-fired generating stations. To generate electricity to export, Hydro-Québec would build hydroelectric projects at dates earlier than those it had scheduled; the more it sold, the sooner it would have to build. Hydro-Québec set itself the goal of negotiating new contracts such that, by century's end, it would be exporting 3,500 megawatts of firm electricity.

Early in 1988, Hydro-Québec had signed two major export contracts. The first was with Central Maine Power, which planned to resell some of the 300 megawatts of firm power it would import to other New England states. (This contract was later cancelled.) The second, for up to 450 megawatts of firm power and firm energy, was with Vermont Joint Owners, a consortium of the major utilities in Vermont. Under this deal, Quebec would be providing as much as half of all the electricity used in Vermont during the 1990s. Finally, Hydro-Québec had also signed an agreement in principle for its largest ever export contract: to sell 1,000 megawatts of firm power over the course of 21 years to the New York Power Authority.[4] By this contract, Quebec would supply about six percent of New York State's electricity needs around the turn of the century. Bourassa boasted that these sales contracts were going to bring in a total revenue of $40-billion in revenue to Hydro-Québec.

Together with existing export contracts, these new deals meant that if all options in all its contracts were exercised, at the end of the century Hydro-Québec would be exporting more than 2,400 megawatts of firm power. This was a good deal less than the 10,000 megawatts of firm power which, according to Bourassa, were needed to launch his Power from the North project. Nonetheless, there was an election coming up, and he needed to show that the scheme he had promoted was being implemented.

In March 1988, Bourassa announced that three new power plants together capable of generating another 2,500 megawatts of electricity would be built at the La Grande complex, along with a new transmission line. These works comprise much of phase two of the La Grande complex.[5] This project, he said proudly, was a manifestation of patriotism, for it would create some 40,000 job-years for Québécois. Though the project was small relative to what he had grandiloquently projected while on the campaign trail, he gave it the resounding title of James Bay II.

In deciding to start work on the second phase of the La Grande complex, Hydro-Québec had advanced its construction schedule. Bourassa wanted the utility to advance its schedule even more. Some senior staff chose to leave the utility, only discreetly hinting at the reasons for their departure. Georges Lafond, who left in 1986, used an alimentary metaphor. "Hydro-Québec," he said "still has to digest James Bay One."[6] Guy Coulombe, who left in 1988, used a nautical metaphor. The president of the utility, he said later that year, should be the captain of the ship, the sole person steering it. The government's role was to set policy directions.[7] Jacques Guevremont succeeded Lafond as executive vice-president in charge of external markets and, in May 1988, Richard Drouin, an old school chum of Bourassa's, became Hydro-Québec's new chief executive.

To increase its firm load Hydro-Québec was not only promoting exports of electricity but also consumption within Quebec. In 1988, under pressure from its political masters, it revised the arrangements by which it had been nakedly subsidizing electricity-hungry industries by offering them cut-rate electricity. Now Hydro-Québec inaugurated a program in which it shares risks and profits with its clients; that is, the price they pay varies with the price they receive for their products. The details of the contracts are secret, but it is clear that Hydro-Québec offered attractively cheap electricity, and thus achieved the same ends as the original program: stimulating the establishment or expansion of new industrial plants. Of the 13 companies which signed up, most processed metals. The largest of the group were aluminum refineries; early in 1989, four aluminum companies made public their plans to invest more than $4-billion in new or expanded smelters.

Hydro-Québec's internal demand has been growing dramatically because, in large part, of the mammoth appetite of such industries for power. (Of all the electricity sold by Hydro-Québec, industry now consumes about a third. By the end of the century industry will consume almost a half, and aluminum smelters alone will consume almost one-fifth of Hydro-Québec's output.)

While demand was growing, due to increases both in exports and in internal sales, Hydro-Québec's supply of electricity was diminishing, due to drought. It now takes almost all the water that runs into Hydro-Québec's reservoirs in years of average precipitation to produce electricity to meet its firm requirements. But between 1985 and 1990, levels of rain and snow in Quebec were below normal. Hydro-Québec, which at the beginning of the decade was swimming in surpluses was driven to expensive measures by the end of the decade such as running its oil-fired generating station during the winters.

To avoid narrowing its margin of manoeuvre even less, Hydro-Québec announced that it would not sign any new contracts to export firm power before the next century. And in March 1989, to increase its margin of manoeuvre further, it announced that it had moved up the scheduled dates for construction of its next two hydroelectric projects: the Great Whale and the Nottaway-Broadback-Rupert complexes. It was going to exploit half of the remaining hydroelectric potential in Quebec. It was going to build James Bay II.

After surging across land that is transitional between tundra and taiga, the river known as Great Whale (Grande rivière de la Baleine, in French) flows into Hudson Bay at a point some 160 kilometres north of the La Grande's mouth. With its many rapids and falls, and its canyons and cliffs, it is a spectacularly beautiful river. And as its name suggests — it is the river that is great; the whales that consort off its mouth are the relatively small beluga — it is big.

Here Hydro-Québec plans to build the Great Whale hydroelectric complex, which it put on hold early in the 1980s, when demand for electricity slowed down. Into the Great Whale River it plans to divert the Little Whale River (Petite rivière de la Baleine) and — in its original plan — partially divert the Nastapoca River. One of the five dams in the complex would increase the area of the lake known as Lac Bienville by one-third, turning it into the highest and biggest reservoir of the complex. Together, all its reservoirs would occupy about 4,400 square kilometres. They would feed water to the three generating stations to be built along the Great Whale River, to produce a maximum of some 3,168 megawatts. To complete the complex by 1998, construction of the access infrastructure — mainly a road running north from the La Grande complex, another road running east-west through the complex, and airports — would have to begin in 1991. (These dates, as we shall see, have been pushed back.) Hydro-Québec estimates the cost of this complex, including the cost of building transmission lines, at $12.6-billion.

After the Great Whale complex, Hydro-Québec plans to build the Nottaway-Broadback-Rupert complex, the last and biggest of the James Bay megaprojects. Planners are juggling with possible configurations of this complex. It is likely that they will divert both the Nottaway and Rupert Rivers into the Broadback, and that they will build 11 power-houses with a combined total capacity of some 8,400 megawatts. The reservoirs backed up behind the 16 dams would occupy a total area of 6,500 square kilometres. Hydro-Québec hopes to complete this by about 2001.

During the 1990s, Hydro-Québec plans to spend some $44-billion building these projects and the six power lines that will carry their electricity south. It is doing so, it says, in order to meet Quebec's needs for electricity.

* * *

Bourassa wants to do with Quebec's water what the Persian Gulf countries do with their oil — turn a large flow of energy into a concentrated flow of money. The money comes from the more than two and a half million bill-paying customers plugged into Hydro-Québec's grid. The money goes to Hydro-Québec, to its lenders, and to its suppliers such as construction and consulting engineering firms in Quebec. These companies, along with the aluminum and other companies favoured by Hydro-Québec's attractive rates, and the American utilities who save by buying its power, all benefit from James Bay II, and they — and politicians such as Bourassa who articulate their interests — are its principal proponents.

After his election in 1985, Bourassa's first trip out of Quebec was to New York City where, seeking political and financial support for hydroelectric development in Quebec, he met with politicians, bureaucrats, and investment bankers. To continue opening doors and mobilizing support among this network, he formed a consultative committee of influential Americans. It includes John Dyson, a former president of the New York Power Authority, and James Schlesinger, a Secretary of Energy in the Carter administration and now a principal in the investment banking firm of Lehman Brothers.

For American utilities, such as the New York Power Authority, the appeal of electricity from Quebec is that it is cheap. Because of its extraordinary endowment of water power, Quebec can generate electricity for less than utilities in the United States can. According to James Schlesinger, in his preface to Bourassa's *Power from the North*, power could be generated at James Bay for five US cents a kilowatthour, half or less the cost of power from new capacity now being brought on line in the United States. The price at which Hydro-Québec sells electricity to the United States is determined by complex formulae to be less than avoided cost — that is, less than the cost of energy from the power station the American utility would have to build or operate if it did not import from Quebec. These savings can be considerable. In a 1988 letter to its shareholders, Green Mountain Power Corporation, a member of the Vermont Joint Owners Consortium, reported it was buying power from Quebec for 30 percent below its next-cheapest supply alternative.

That importing electricity from Quebec means not burning fossil fuels which would have contributed to acid rain and the greenhouse effect, or that it is less trouble to arrange an import deal than to build a new power plant, or that hydroelectricity is renewable, or that the 1988 free trade agreement between Canada and the United States increases American confidence that the electricity will flow across the border without government restriction — these advantages are touted by publicists on both sides of the border, but they are icing on the cake: the key attraction of power from James Bay II is its price. For investment banking firms such as Lehman Brothers the attraction of James Bay II is financial too. These firms will collect commissions of about 1.7 percent from the sale of Hydro-Québec bonds; and, to pay for James Bay II, Hydro-Québec will be borrowing, over the next decade, more money than any other company in Canada.

For the lenders, for institutions such as insurance and pension funds that hold really big money, such bonds are an attractive long-term investment, yielding a sure and steady return. What inspires their confidence is the abundance and unceasing flow of the water Hydro-Québec controls, the assurance that the investment in this water power is sheltered from inflation, and the utility's demonstrated competence in turning flowing water into electricity and hence into cash.

Abundant Quebec's water power certainly is. Analysts at the New York investment banking firm of Kidder, Peabody and Company once calculated that the energy that will pour from Hydro-Québec's existing reservoirs into its grid over the course of the next half-century — the useful life of a hydroelectric facility — is more than twice Canada's total proven oil and gas reserves, and greater than the combined proven oil and gas reserves of the ten largest energy companies in the United States, including Exxon, Mobil, and Gulf Oil.[8]

Inflation makes uncertain the return on an investment in, say, a coal-fired plant. The price of coal, and of labour, can rise, eroding profits. But almost all the costs of building and running a hydroelectric project are the initial costs of building dams, powerhouses, transmission lines. Once the huge amounts of capital these require have been raised, further expenses are negligible. Running a hydroelectric plant takes no fuel, and almost no labour and, once built, the project supplies electricity for its 50 of more years of useful life. Investment in hydroelectricity, in other words, is safe from inflation.

These investments are made safe, too, by the guarantee of the province of Quebec that the loans will be repaid. The provincial government has the power either to tax the people it governs or, through Hydro-Québec, to increase the price of electricity charged its captive market. To assure that the flow of money to its creditors continues, it does both.

Of all the proponents of James Bay II, the largest is Hydro-Québec. Its $36-billion in assets made it the third-largest company in Canada in 1990, and one of the largest public utilities on the continent. Its revenues from sales amount to almost $6-billion per year. It has almost 23,000 employees, more than most other enterprises in Quebec. For the elite of the generation that graduated since the *Révolution tranquille* it has been a source of prestigious and high-paying jobs. The corporate culture of the utility is one in which career ambitions are satisfied, empires built, and power exercised in borrowing for large hydroelectric projects, and in building them. The staff of Hydro-Québec has a collective interest in James Bay II; this project assures their privileged social and financial future.

Some of the most vociferous proponents of James Bay II are the suppliers of Hydro-Québec, the businesses and labour groups — it includes the Quebec Manufacturers Association and the Quebec Federation of Labour — who collectively form what has been called the bulldozer coalition. Up to 80 percent of the money spent on hydroelectric development in Quebec is spent within the province. Following its *achat chez nous* policy — its policy of preferring to buy services and equipment from suppliers with headquarters in Quebec — Hydro-Québec has been pumping into the provincial economy amounts that rise above $2-billion per year when in the thick of hydroelectric project construction. It is far and away the biggest single spender in Quebec; of every $20 spent in

Quebec, Hydro-Québec spends at least $1 and, in years of most active construction, sometimes as many as $5.

This flow of money is channelled to consulting engineering firms; to manufacturers of turbines, generators, towers, transformers and the like; to construction companies; to suppliers of cement and construction materials; to truckers; and to related unions. (Indirectly, Hydro-Québec's expenditures support more than 30,000 jobs in Quebec.) No construction firm wants to have millions of dollars worth of heavy equipment sit idle in its yards. Engineering firms want projects for their highly-paid staff to design. All these firms depend heavily on Hydro-Québec expenditures, and want them to continue, as do their employees. Some of these firms exercise considerable political power, and none more so than the engineering firm Lavalin.

The contract to manage the construction of the La Grande complex in conjunction with Bechtel catapulted Groupe Lavalin into the big league of multinational consulting engineering and construction firms. I talked once to Marcel Dufour who, along with Bernard Lamarre and Armand Couture, was one of the four founders and owners of the firm. "At James Bay," he told me, "we learned how to manage very large projects. We knew all the players, and we knew the score." Using the years of steady income from its James Bay contract, Lavalin expanded. It bought firms offering know-how in a wide variety of fields: environmental research, economics, mapping, geotechnical studies and more. It built up a pool of expertise and of connections: Lavalin hired some of the smartest and best-connected of former provincial and federal cabinet ministers. It evolved into the largest engineering conglomerate in Canada, and one of the largest in the world: a kind of supermarket at which clients from around the world could shop for things like city plans or oil refineries. With SNC, the rival engineering firm which it had out-manoeuvred in winning the James Bay project management contract, and others, it prepared preliminary studies of the Three Gorges dam project on the Yangtze River in China (which, if built, would be the most colossal hydroelectric project the world has ever seen, and would displace more than a million people).

During the last generation, Quebec has grown increasingly materialistic, and entrepreneurs have replaced the technocrats of Hydro-Québec as popular heroes. Few entrepreneurs were perceived as being more successful, were more fawned over by public and press, more lauded as a symbol of Quebec's world-beating vigour, than Bernard Lamarre, the founder and principal owner of Lavalin. Lamarre believed in the grandiose, in bigness for the sake of bigness. His firm diversified widely, into health care, broadcasting, real estate and more.

Lamarre felt that Lavalin could do everything and anything. He was wrong. In the 1990s, Lavalin became strapped for cash. Its core engineering business was doing well, but not some of its many subsidiaries, to buy which it had gone heavily into debt. A deal by which a Lavalin acquisition (run by Armand Couture) would build and operate an elevated commuter rail system in Bangkok fell through. So, disastrously, did a deal to buy 12 used aircraft at $60-million apiece, and resell them to Aeroflot, the Soviet airline. Lavalin collapsed. Lamarre lost his empire, and in the fall of 1991, SNC, with the help of the provincial government, bought his engineering firm, and fused with it to form SNC-Lavalin. With some 6,000 employees, this new creation is ten times larger than the next biggest engineering firm in Quebec.

SNC-Lavalin's president, Guy Saint-Pierre, was a member of the Liberal government in the early 1970s, and collaborated with Bourassa on launching the La Grande complex. Without James Bay power, he said at the time, "we would be in possession of a true museum, with picturesque fishermen half-living on government hand-outs and some tourist attractions. We will have birds and fresh water, and vegetables and animal reserves. But will we abandon our televisions, bungalows, electric kitchens, movie theatres, autos, planes, modern apartments, our modern life to enter the post-industrial age backwards?"[9] Big firms need big projects, and one of the big projects that SNC-Lavalin hopes to work on is the Great Whale complex. Before their fusion, the James Bay Energy Corporation had already promised Lavalin a 50 percent share and SNC a 35 percent share of engineering management work at the Great Whale complex.

What characterizes the proponents of James Bay II is their common and considerable financial interest in the project. They also share ideas about the environmental and social impacts of the James Bay project. Environmental groups, according to Bourassa, are merely making a few cries of hesitation and caution, and he and other proponents dismiss the potential contribution of energy efficiency. "The fundamental question," Bourassa has said, "is not whether to build Great Whale, but whether we will choose nuclear, coal or hydroelectric power. You don't have to be a Nobel prizewinner to know that a hydro plant protects the environment better than a coal-fired or a nuclear plant. To be convinced of that, you just have to go to Three Mile Island or Chernobyl."[10]

The benefits the project provides far outweigh whatever minor, local damage it causes, say the proponents, and some of these benefits flow to the Natives. The project speeds up the inevitable modernization of the Natives' outmoded way of life. "They cannot avoid change for ever," Jacques Guevremont has said. "I don't believe the Native peoples want to live in the Stone Age. I don't want to live like my great-grandfather lived. But the Natives complain too much. All they want is more money. They are not saying positive things."[11]

"How can the Crees talk about genocide?" Guevremont, and other James Bay II proponents, ask. "Look at their birth rate. They are reproducing, in fact, faster than the French Canadians, faster than most other peoples in the world. They signed an agreement allowing us to develop the whole territory. Let us talk rationally. Hydroelectric development will not harm the Crees; it will create the jobs they need."

What characterizes the proponents, too, is a taste for the grandiose, and an ideology which blends technological optimism with a utilitarian view of nature. They are the kind of people who would make real the metaphor Spaceship Earth, who would engineer all natural ecosystems so as to manage them for human gain. They propose continental scale improvements to the planet's energy and water systems. That the James Bay rivers should be turned to electricity to feed the world's hungriest and greediest energy markets and that James Bay itself should become the continent's water tank, are, in their macro-vision of things, rational and inevitable rearrangements. Camille Dagenais, former head of SNC, once summed up their ideas and values for me. "In my view," he explained, "nature is awful, and what we do is cure it."[12]

NOTES

1. Fraser, *PQ*.
2. Robert Bourassa, interview with author, Montreal, 13 April 1985.
3. Bourassa, *Power from the North*, 18.
4. The initial contract with Vermont Joint Owners was for up to 450 megawatts of firm power and for a total of 62 terawatthours of firm energy to be delivered between 1990 to 2020. These amounts have subsequently been reduced. Hydro-Québec signed its two contracts with the New York Power Authority in April 1989. One is for the largest block of firm power Hydro-Québec had ever exported; for 21 years, between 1995 and 2016, it guarantees to deliver 1,000 megawatts of firm power and a total of 130 terawatthours of firm energy to the New York Power Authority, which in turn plans to resell most of this power to utilities in the southern part of the state; it plans, for example, to sell about half the power to Consolidated Edison for use in New York City.
5. Phase Two of the La Grande Complex, now under construction, consists of the three powerhouses, La Grande-1, Brisay, and Laforge, whose construction was announced in 1988, and LG-2A the additional powerhouse being built beside the La Grande-2 power station. When all these are completed, around 1995, the total generating capacity of the La Grande complex will be 14,791 megawatts.

6. *Hydro-Presse* (Hydro-Québec), mid-September 1986. (My translation.)
7. Bombardier, "Guy Coulombe."
8. Bourassa, *Power from the North*, 78.
9. Richardson, *Strangers Devour the Land*, 328.
10. *The Montreal Gazette*, 16 July 1991.
11. Jacques Guevremont, "Daybreak" (CBC Radio, Montreal), 28 February 1990.
12. Camille Dagenais, interview with author, Montreal, 11 December 1985.

CHAPTER 9

Opponents

In his foreword to Bourassa's book *Power from the North*, James Schlesinger compared the James Bay project to the Panama canal and the Alaska pipeline. "We have become blasé about such great achievements," he wrote. "Regrettably, we have lost a feeling of awe." In fact, what many people feel about the James Bay project is awe, in one of the original senses of the word: an overwhelming sense of fear of that which is powerful.

One of these people is John Petagumscum, a short, powerfully-built man in his 70s with a scruff of chin-whiskers, a shock of wiry black hair, and hands like weathered tools. He lives at the mouth of the Great Whale River in the Cree half, Whapmagoostui (the place where there are whales), of a twin village whose Inuit half is called Kuujjuarapik (big little river).[1] Petagumscum is a former chief of Whapmagoostui and a respected hunter. He is, he says, a descendant of a great shaman who saved his people from famine by killing one of the rare and elusive fresh water seals.

Since the Ice Age isolated them from the sea, these seals have lived in lakes at the headwaters of the Nastapoca River. Unlike their salt water relatives, these inland seals eat only fish and, according to Petagumscum, have a delicious fishy taste. Scientists wrangle over whether they are a subspecies or just a variety of the harbour seal. What is special about the fresh water seal, for Petagumscum, is that "although it was hard to hunt, it saved the lives of entire families at times past when famine struck. When all else was not available, by miracle a hunter killed a fresh water seal. It was as if the Creator planned it this way." He took his first fresh water seal on the day his first son was born. Religiously, he takes one seal himself each year, in order to ensure that after he dies this tradition may continue, he has taught one of his sons how to hunt these animals.

The original plans for the Great Whale complex call for a partial diversion of the Nastapoca, which would cause water level to fluctuate in the lakes these rare seals inhabit. Petagumscum has spoken about his fears that these changes will hurt the health of the seals. He has spoken, too, about the dried up rivers and the valleys that will be flooded by the Great Whale complex, and the beaver, otter, marten and mink and other animals it will kill; about the waterfowl who will lose their nesting sites on small islands, where they are protected from predators; about the disease that will strike all the animals because of the new things that will be in the water; about devastating effects on the hunting and trapping life. "It will mean the end of us as a people," he says.

He feels not only fear but also anger, because the hydroelectric project will show disrespect to what in his eyes are sacred gifts. "You see," he explains, "the land is precious to the Crees because it is their life…It is the garden of life for the Crees given to them to use by the Creator."[2]

Petagumscum's fears are typical of those of Cree elders, the traditional leaders and the guardians of the old hunting culture. They are shared and articulated by the educated, urbanized and politically sophisticated young leaders.

In 1987, the Crees of Quebec elected as their Grand Chief the former chief of Mistissini, Matthew Coon-Come, with the mandate of opposing hydroelectric development, a mandate which soon became focused on delaying and blocking the Great Whale complex. Coon-Come has established his credentials both in the city and in the bush. He was born in the bush, and spent the long winters as a child in hunting camps with his family. When he was six years old, he remembers, a white cleric in a black robe pulled him from his mother, stuffed him into a bush plane with 20 other crying kids, and took them all on a four-hour flight away to school.

He learned to resent non-Natives — for, among other things, forbidding him to speak Cree in school — but not to be cowed by them: he made a name for himself, as a boy, by pushing the son of a white preacher off a dock. Coon-Come did well in school, and went on to study courses of interest to him, including administration and political science at, among other universities, McGill in Montreal. Home in Mistissini, in 1974, at a meeting to decide whether to approve the agreement in principle that had been negotiated, urged by other youths, he spoke at length about his feelings for the land, and his support for the agreement, and received an ovation for his eloquence. "Son," his father said to him, "you talk like a white man." Guided by his father, Coon-Come went back to the land to become an authentic Cree, spending a full year in the bush.[3]

Coon-Come, who is 35 years old, is an effective spokesman for the Crees: photogenic — slim, good bones, a radiant smile —and an articulate and passionate orator. When he speaks, he evokes happy pictures of his culture. He tells, for instance, how his father would cut certain parts from the beaver, moose or goose they were about to eat, put it in the fire, and chant a song of thanks to the animal and of hope for future success in hunting. He speaks about the quandary of the Crees, with their growing population, and he fulminates against the James Bay project and the agreement that, as a youth, he had supported.

"The land cannot support all these people as hunters and trappers, especially when it is being destroyed by hydroelectric development. In the villages there are no jobs either. The rivers are dammed, the electricity is exported, and we're left with nothing. It's a situation that makes young people very frustrated and angry."

"We wish we had never signed the James Bay agreement. Its terms have not been honoured. You might as well just put a stone around our necks and drown us in the reservoirs."

James Bay II, he has said, "will cause considerable erosion, alter the seasonal patterns and quantity of water flow in the concerned rivers and water basins, adversely affect the wildlife and marine resources of Hudson Bay and of James Bay, including marine mammals and fish, flood the nesting and feeding sites of waterfowl, including migratory birds, destroy the habitat of fur-bearing animals, change the migration routes and adversely affect caribou, destroy spawning areas of fish, deplete subsistence food resources upon which we depend, severely increase mercury contamination of fish, change the ecology of Hudson Bay and of James Bay, endanger a very fragile environment, threaten endangered species, cause substantial pollution, endanger the health, safety and welfare of the Native population and interfere with and cause extensive and irreparable damage, loss and prejudice to our livelihood, our way of life and our traditional use of the land and natural resources."

"Why spend billions of dollars to destroy the environment and to destroy my people just to export electricity to the United States? Does this make any sense?"

"We are fighting for our survival. Aboriginal nations have been pushed aside for too long. The problem with Bourassa's dream is that it is fast becoming an environmental and economic nightmare."[4]

Coon-Come's Inuit counterpart is Charlie Watts, who was the chief Inuit negotiator of the James Bay and Northern Québec Agreement and is now, among other things, a member of the Canadian senate and president of the Inuit regional administration. Relations between the Crees and Inuit have been strained in the past, during the negotiations of the Agreement, and continue to be strained. Very few Inuit use lands to be flooded by James Bay II, or used lands that were flooded by the La Grande complex. A majority of the Inuit have, through elections, given to Charlie Watts a mandate to negotiate for compensation from the Great Whale project: for jobs, money, and more self-government. Because of his compliancy, some Cree refer to Watts as "Senator Megawatts." The three dissident Inuit communities remain flatly opposed to the James Bay project and to the agreements it spawned. The only Inuit who stand to be directly affected by the Great Whale complex, those who live in Kuujjuarapik, at the mouth of the Great Whale River, join their Cree neighbours in opposing it.[5]

The developers say that the Natives of northern Quebec, in signing the James Bay and Northern Québec Agreement, have already consented to, and accepted compensation for, the building of the James Bay II hydroelectric complexes. Both the Great Whale and the Nottaway-Broad-back-Rupert complexes are described in that agreement, and referring to them, a key clause in the text reads: "It is agreed that these known projects and any additions and/or substantial modifications to Le Complex La Grande (1975), if built, shall be considered as future projects subject to the environmental regime only in respect to ecological impacts and that sociological factors or impacts shall not be grounds for the Cree and/or Inuit to oppose or prevent the said developments." Though tortured, these words say, clearly enough, that the Crees promise not to raise political objections to James Bay II.

The pattern of accommodation, in which the Natives concede to the developers and take compensation, will continue, the developers believe. They point out that the Crees signed the La Grande Agreement (1986). In this, the latest amendment to the James Bay and Northern Québec Agreement, the Crees consented to construction of three new powerhouses in the second phase of the La Grande complex, and to construction of the direct current transmission line; in exchange, they accepted compensation of $110-million, and a promise that Hydro-Québec would hire and train 150 Crees to work on its hydroelectric project.

The developers are cynical about the Crees' current protests. The Crees promised not to oppose further projects, the developers complain, and they believe that Cree talk about environmental disaster and cultural genocide is hollow exaggeration, a bargaining ploy designed to raise the compensation — which, according to the developers' latest offer, stands at $1-billion. They are confident that this amount will buy the eventual and inevitable compliance of the Crees.

Matthew Coon-Come and others point to the self-suppressing clause in the James Bay and Northern Québec Agreement as proof that it was signed under duress. The compensation moneys already received were for the La Grande complex, not for James Bay II, they say. The Crees say they signed the 1986 supplementary agreement, consenting to further development on the La Grande, only because it was already a ruined river. The job offers contained in that agreement do not help them, for their young people refuse to work for Hydro-Québec, and anyway very few speak French, a necessary qualification for such jobs. They flatly refuse to negotiate with Hydro-Québec about the Great Whale project. Talk with us first about the promises made in the James Bay and Northern Québec Agreement and never honoured, they say. Their chief lawyer, James O'Reilly, has calculated that because of these broken promises the Crees are already owed $1-billion. They are angered at talk of money for accepting James Bay II. What they want is to own and control the land and all its resources, including the rivers that Hydro-Québec, without their consent, is exploiting.

The Crees believe they have been and are being wronged. As the words of both Petagumscum and Coon-Come show, they see the fight over the

Great Whale complex as a battle between the forces of good and those of evil. They also calculate that this is a fight from which they can lose little and, possibly, gain much. Their current stance redeems them in the eyes of those — especially other Indians — who maligned them for renouncing their aboriginal rights. In the long term, they will probably gain, either by accepting some form of compensation, as the developers expect, or by winning sovereignty, as the developers fear. Meanwhile, they have a large population of frustrated youth, for whom opposing James Bay II has become a national project, a means of affirming their independence and their merit — much the same function, in fact, as building hydroelectric projects served the Québécois during the *Révolution tranquille*.

The conflict over the Great Whale project is not a replay of that over the La Grande complex. Although the proponents, and their arguments for the James Bay project, have not changed significantly, the number and vigour of the opponents has, as has the persuasive force of their arguments against the project. The Crees have more money, confidence, experience, and contacts than they had a generation ago. Just as the developers rely on knowledge and connections held by consulting engineering firms, so the Crees rely on a network of experts. Some of the Crees' advisers have been with them since the fight over the La Grande complex. James O'Reilly is still their principal lawyer. Brian Craik, a former anthropologist and a fluent speaker of Cree, is their Ottawa-based government liaison man. Alan Penn is their principal environmental adviser. Among the new generation of their advisers are lawyers Robert and Johanne Mainville and Ian Goodman of Boston, a young and brilliantly numerate energy analyst. These and other people help plan and wage the Crees' legal and political battles, shape public opinion in their favour, and provide the ideas with which they are challenging the developers.

The Crees are not just defending their culture and environment; both in Quebec and in the United States they and their advisers are challenging current energy and economic policies, and proposing alternatives.

They have many supporters, on both sides of the border. The fundamental difference between the current dispute and that of twenty years ago is the extent to which thoughts and feelings that were dismissed a generation ago as the motley notions of counterculture cranks are now creditable. Environmental concerns have moved from the margin towards the mainstream of politics. So, too, has sympathy with Native peoples, and guilt about their treatment by industrial society.

There are two reasons why non-Natives sympathize with the Crees' fight against the James Bay project, and more generally, with the fight of aboriginal peoples around the world for survival and for justice. One reason is the selfless impulse of decent people to side with the underdog, and thus to feel anger with the intrusion of industrial society, embodied in the James Bay project, into the lives of the Natives of northern Quebec.

The second reason is the hope that if the Crees and other indigenous peoples were to exercise control over more of the land they claim, they might slow the growing despoliation of the planet. This hope is based on a notion made explicit in the influential 1987 Bruntland Report on the Global Economy and the Environment: that Native peoples have accumulated wisdom over thousands of years of living as part of nature, and are therefore well-equipped to be its stewards.

The environmental movement, which is opposed to Natives on issues such as fur-trapping and whaling, has joined forces with them to fight issues such as the James Bay project. Both those working to protect the environment and those working to protect indigenous cultures share scepticism about the imperatives of economic growth, and are convinced that it would be environmentally, socially, and economically preferable to invest in energy efficiency rather than in greater energy supplies.

* * *

The handful of militant Quebecers who opposed the James Bay project, and had been articulating such ideas ever since it was launched, continued their fight, even though the Natives rejected their support, and even though public support — never strong — for their position, and for the Natives' position, dwindled after the signing of the James Bay and Northern Québec Agreement. Most Quebecers thought that the Agreement had resolved the Natives' grievances, and that the project was a success.

Hélène Lajambe tried to convince them otherwise. The project had become an obsession for her, as it was for Robert Bourassa. It was the subject of her master's and doctoral theses in economics, of her many articles and press releases, and of the critical quotes for which journalists, seeking balance in their pieces, relied on her. One of her many arguments was that building the James Bay project had effectively starved the manufacturing sector of capital. This made Quebecers worse off; relative to Canadian averages, unemployment in Quebec was higher and per person income rates lower. Hydro-Québec had grossly over-invested and, in order to repay its mounting debt, was caught in a vicious circle, constrained to borrow, build, and sell ever more power at ridiculously cheap rates. Bourassa was turning Quebec into an economically dependent Third World nation. Quebec, and its American customers, should mount programs to save electricity. Doing so would provide energy more cheaply and create more jobs than building dams or importing their power. Quebec should hold a public debate on its energy policy.[6]

When she delivered her message to a meeting of Hydro-Québec managers, one of them, Simon Paré, who was then responsible for Hydro-Québec's sales to New York, replied by sending her a candle, and accused her of wanting to send Quebec back to the pre-electricity dark ages.

What began to change public opinion — on both sides of the border — about the James Bay project, was the building of power lines. As they came south, these lines brought a concrete manifestation of what had been a remote and hence ignored project into people's back yards, where they did not want it, and gave them a bitter taste of what the Natives had to swallow.

In the mid-1980s, Hydro-Québec began building its direct current power line through the Eastern Townships (or Estrie) region of Quebec — a place of peaceful towns, dairy farms, small logging operations, and the like — to the border with Vermont. Bruce Aikman, a farmer and engineer, raised the alarm after seeing surveyors near his land, and learning from American newspapers where the power lines would likely pass. A fight ensued between citizens' groups and the utility. People were scared that electromagnetic fields from the lines would cause calves to be still-born, or worse.[7] They were scared of the herbicides with which Hydro-Québec clears the underbrush in its transmission corridors. They were angry because Hydro-Québec would not compensate people adequately for the decrease its power lines caused in the value of their land. The citizens lost. Hydro-Québec, Aikman told me, "was arrogant, contemptuous of the public, and tried to mislead."[8]

There was another kerfuffle when Hydro-Québec wanted the power line to cross the Saint Lawrence River strung from giant pylons which would disfigure a region of exceptional beauty. This time the citizens won; the power line crosses the river underground, through a tunnel.

These conflicts eroded public confidence in Hydro-Québec, as did its frequent power failures and its increases in electricity rates. Hydro-Québec no longer played the role of national icon. When James Bay II was an-nounced, more Quebecers were receptive to the critics' arguments against it than had been a generation ago, and though nationalist sentiment was growing, it no longer implied unquestioning support for Hydro-Québec; many nationalists could — and do — oppose the Great Whale project.

A grassroots movement in Quebec against James Bay II began to coalesce at the Green Energy Conference which Hélène Lajambe (shortly before she returned to her native France), Gordon Edwards (president of the Canadian Coalition for Nuclear Responsibility) and others organized in Montreal in 1989. Volunteers began making telephone calls and attending meetings, writing letters to newspaper editors, getting signatures on petitions, organizing demonstrations, amassing information, forming groups, soliciting support. In Quebec, the Coalition for a Public Debate on Energy includes church, union, consumer, environmental, Native and other groups to which, it is claimed, one-sixth the population of the province belongs. It demands a moratorium on James Bay II, and a public debate. This demand is echoed by national groups such as the Ottawa-based Cultural Survival (Canada) — a spin-off from a project launched by Harvard anthropologists to defend Native peoples and their environment from industrial development, and the Canadian Arctic Resources Committee — which works to protect the environment and encourage Native participation in decisions about development in the North, as well as international organizations such as Greenpeace and Friends of the Earth.

Americans have always been central players in developing Quebec's hydroelectricity. American capitalists owned the first hydroelectric plants here. It was in the United States that Quebec borrowed the money with which it bought the privately owned electric utilities, and much of the money with which it built the La Grande complex. American experts were key in managing and building this complex.

Now Hydro-Québec's zeal to export to the States has connected citizens there to the James Bay project in ways the utility did not anticipate and does not like, since the flow of electricity to the south has triggered a counterflow of ideas and challenges to the north. American citizens, whose tradition of democratic participation in decisions on environmental and other public questions is far stronger than that of Quebecers or of Canadians, first became involved in the James Bay project because of power lines. A group of citizens known by the acronym PROTECT — Prudent Residents Opposed To Electrical Cable Transmission — formed to protest the Marcy-South power line, which the New York Power Authority built through primarily rural and scenic areas to carry power, imported under the terms of its 1982 agreement with Hydro-Québec, towards New York City.

Hydro-Québec's deal with Central Maine Power required building a huge transmission line through Maine, which would cross the Appalachian trail, and much wild mountain country. A group, No Thank Q Hydro-Quebec, campaigned against the power line and the contract; it claimed a victory when, in January 1989, the Maine Public Utilities Commission, the state regulatory body, rejected the contract because the Maine utility had not proven that importing electricity from Quebec would be cheaper than options such as investing in improvements in energy efficiency.

Because the contracts Hydro-Québec signed in the late 1980s with New York and Vermont triggered the utility's decision to advance its schedule for constructing James Bay II, groups sprang up in these States to campaign against the contracts, and against the fresh assault on the taiga and the Crees entailed by Hydro-Québec's need to generate power to meet these contracts. In Vermont, for example, Jim Higgins, a social worker who has canoed in the James Bay area, helped form the New England Energy Efficiency Coalition. In New York City, Jeff Wollock of the Solidarity Foundation — which puts royalties earned by the Irish rock band U2 to work in defence of Native peoples — helped found the James Bay Defense Coalition, which comprises some 20 organizations, and began lobbying politicians to cancel the New York Power Authority contracts. Major international environmental organizations became involved. In July 1989 the New York-based National Audubon Society publicized, in Quebec, its concerns that water resource developments would harm the large numbers of migratory birds that use the James Bay coast, and called for full, public environmental hearings. The Sierra Club created an umbrella organization, the James Bay and Northern Quebec Task Force, and channeled funds through a think-tank founded by Hélène Lajambe, the Centre d'analyse des politiques énergétiques, to establish an office with a one-person staff in Montreal. The large organizations have not swallowed up the grassroots movement. There are at least 30 anti-James Bay II groups on college campuses throughout New York State, and more elsewhere in the Northeast.

Some groups in the United States have a commercial interest in opposing imports of electricity from Quebec. Coal-mining interests in states such as Pennsylvania and North Dakota, for example, complain that imported hydroelectricity competes with domestic coal in the energy marketplace. Hydro-Québec also competes with some of the small companies which have sprung up in the United States after passage of a law in 1978 obliging utilities to buy power at a fair price from non-utility generators. Some of these companies produce electricity from, among other things, small hydroelectric plants, and boilers burning wood or municipal trash. Others co-generate: that is, they produce steam not only for internal needs — for production processes in some industrial plants, for example, or for space heating in schools or shopping malls — but also to generate electricity for sale to utilities and distribution through the power grid. The opposition of such interests, however, has carried little political clout relative to that of disinterested citizens' groups.

The activists opposing the Great Whale project in Canada and in the United States tend to be young, dedicated, selfless, hard-working, well-educated and self-confident. Most are information junkies; their principal tools are the telephone, computer, and fax machine. They are ideologically various — they include anti-nuclear activists, bioregionalists, eco-feminists, leftists, human rights activists, and peaceniks. What they agree on are their three main arguments against James Bay II: one, that it will damage the environment and hence the Indians severely, unnecessarily, and unfairly; two, that it makes dubious economic sense; and three, that managing the demand for power is an economically and environmentally preferable alternative to building electricity-supplying megaprojects, and to importing power from them.

* * *

What impacts will James Bay II have on the environment and on the Indians? Critics answer with a long catalogue of concerns, some of which I have reported above in listing the concerns of John Petagumscum and Matthew Coon-Come. Other concerns include the probability that, because of the increase in discharge in winter from the mouth of the Great Whale River, there will no longer be ice on the water route the Natives use to travel north along the James Bay coast. In addition, building a road to Great Whale will, for the first time, connect an Inuit community in northern Quebec to urban civilization.

Compared to the impacts of the Great Whale complex, those of the Nottaway-Broadback-Rupert complex would, for a number of reasons, be far more severe. The shallow reservoirs formed by diverting the Nottaway and Rupert Rivers, and damming the Broadback, would flood about twice the area of the Great Whale reservoirs. The NBR complex would destroy more southern, and hence more biologically productive habitat — a forested zone, used by moose, woodland caribou and beaver, among other wildlife, and heavily harvested by the Crees, whose population is most concentrated in this zone. Since there is more forest here than at the La Grande or Great Whale complexes, more mercury would be released when the reservoirs are flooded. The Broadback River's flow would increase tremendously, causing erosion. In the areas where the future reservoirs are planned, loggers are now crudely clear-cutting these forests. The roads built into the hydroelectric complex would give easy access to non-Natives to any hunting and fishing territory that survives.

The damage done by James Bay II, the critics suggest, may have continental or even global repercussions. One way this could happen is by increasing emissions of greenhouse gases. Since growing trees extract carbon dioxide from the air, cutting them or flooding them would lead to a build-up of this gas in the atmosphere, and hence, through the so-called greenhouse effect, to warming of the planet. Worse, when drowned trees rot under water, they release both carbon dioxide and methane, a potent greenhouse gas. Ian Goodman, the energy analyst who consults for the Crees, has calculated that per unit of energy generated, the James Bay hydroelectric projects, and particularly the NBR complex, result in a net increase of greenhouse gases that is at least as much as that attributable to building a coal-burning power plant.

Another way in which James Bay II could have widespread repercussions is by harming habitat critical to migrating birds. Every year, in spring and again in fall, several million migrating birds flock to the intertidal flats and salt marshes of the James Bay coast, and particularly to Rupert's Bay, into which the Nottaway, Broadback and Rupert Rivers drain. They include geese such as the Snow Goose, Canada Goose, and Brant; ducks such as the Green-winged Teal, Black Duck, Mallard, Pintail, and Scaup: and shore birds such as Dunlin, Plovers, Sandpipers, and Yellowlegs. They come to feast on the dense swarms of mosquitoes and biting flies, on the clams, and on the underwater grasses. For these tremendous travellers, many of which winter in South America and most of which summer in the tundra, the coast of James Bay is a major refueling stop.

Many people fear that James Bay II would do more than just double the damage done at the La Grande complex. By an accumulation of disturbances, each relatively innocuous in itself, it may shift ecological balances past the point at which stability can be restored. The habitats about which people worry most are the scientifically almost unknown ones of the coasts and waters of James Bay and Hudson Bay.

Herds of beluga whales — small, strikingly white creatures which, because of their underwater chirping, sailors called "sea canaries" — return every summer to the estuaries of some of the rivers emptying into the east side of Hudson Bay. They do not come to feed or calve but — an Inuit hunter explained to me — to peel off their skins. They lie in low water and rub themselves, leaving cut shards of their skin on the sand and gravel, and frolic. Many are known as individuals to the Inuit and Crees who hunt them, and to the wildlife biologists who study them; they can be identified by the characteristic bullet scars — from hunters who missed — on their backs. The beluga which gave the Great Whale River its name are gone from its estuary; a commercial hunt, organized by the Hudson's Bay Company, wiped them out. But beluga still gather in the estuary of the Little Whale River, which will be cut off by the Great Whale complex, and several hundred come to the mouth of the Nastapoca River.

Quebec is not alone in disturbing this maritime ecosystem. Manitoba and Ontario, the provinces which share the western coasts of James Bay and Hudson Bay, are also planning hydroelectric projects which will amplify the impacts of James Bay II. When the dams are built, far more fresh water will flow into James Bay in winter than did before, and far less in spring. How will this affect the algae that grow under ice in winter and bloom in spring, and that form one of the bottom layers of a food pyramid whose upper layers include birds, seals, beluga, and humans? How will the changes in salinity affect the dense beds of eelgrass on which the Brant geese feed, and which seem to require precise brackish conditions to flourish? Can the food-producing processes in this linked system of marshes, each with its own mix of plants and its own pattern of varying salinity over the year, adapt to alterations in the seasonal rhythm with which rivers have been pouring fresh water into salt water ever since the last Ice Age? How will the mercury injected into this ecosystem affect its creatures? Will ocean currents carry repercussions of disruptions in James Bay to Hudson Strait, the channel connecting Hudson Bay to the

Atlantic, one of the most productive areas in the Arctic; will effects be felt to the south, on the Grand Banks of Newfoundland?

Everybody agrees there would be changes, but nobody can say, with much conviction, what the biological significance of these changes would be. Some conjecture that the consequences on life of these changes will be disastrous. Jan Beyea, for instance, Senior Staff Scientist with the New-York based National Audubon Society, says that "in terms of wildlife and habitat, James Bay is the northern equivalent of the destruction of the tropical rain forest."[9] He has likened Hydro-Québec, which is planning to build James Bay II rapidly, to a drunken teenager driving at 80 miles per hour; even though no one has, as yet been killed, the driver should be stopped. What is happening, some say, is that James Bay and Hudson Bay are being used as a laboratory for an outrageously irresponsible experiment. The results of this experiment will not be known until damage is done. As yet, there is no procedure for a comprehensive, independent review of the impacts of the Great Whale complex — mainly because of jurisdictional squabbles between Ottawa and Quebec — let alone a procedure to review the cumulative impacts of James Bay II and of other projects on the James Bay and Hudson Bay bioregion.

As in all classic battles over the environment, James Bay II pits those who want to preserve habitat and wildlife, against those who want economic growth. As usual in such battles, the environmentalists question the need for the development.

* * *

Does building James Bay II make economic sense for Quebec? Would it stimulate economic development? Would it make Quebec into the wealthiest society in North America, as Bourassa promised it would?

Certainly the flow of investment into the James Bay project has economic effects that ripple through the Quebec economy. Most of the enormous amount of capital spent on building the hydroelectric projects is spent in Quebec, benefitting Hydro-Québec and its suppliers, the engineering, construction, and electrical parts firms. The low rates Hydro-Québec charges electricity-intensive industries encourages them to build large plants such as aluminum refineries. This induces more jobs and business, both in building and in running these plants. To generate booms in these sectors of the economy through capital spending is the *raison d'être* of the Great Whale project and of James Bay II.

It this a sensible way to engender economic development and benefit Quebecers as a whole? No, say Hydro-Québec's critics, for a host of reasons.

Hydroelectric developments are about the most capital intensive of all possible investments; they require enormous amounts of money, and hardly any labour. Construction jobs at the La Grande complex cost, on average, over $320,000 per job-year.[10] These jobs were temporary — they ended when the building boom was over — and they were in the North, so workers had to leave their families.

The La Grande project also induced jobs, both in upstream industries — those that supply goods and services to the construction project — and in downstream industries — those powered by the hydroelectricity. Quebec has not developed a strong industry manufacturing the turbines, power transformers, and other gear for hydroelectric projects. Quebec branches of multinational firms import such technology, and although the money paid for such goods is spent in Quebec, much of it quickly leaves the province. The upstream industries in Quebec that actually benefit from hydroelectric construction are the engineering and construction companies.

The main downstream development stimulated by Quebec's abundant electricity is the aluminum and magnesium refining industry. By calculating how much more Hydro-Québec would get if it sold to the United States the electricity it sells to the Quebec-based aluminum refiners — they pay little, especially relative to the export market — economist Jean-Thomas Bernard estimates that each of the jobs created at these refineries is created with a typical effective subsidy of some $300,000 per year.[11] These plants pollute, and there is little economic activity in Quebec downstream of them; most of the ingots are exported, hence other economies benefit from jobs in plants that process the aluminum.

Do Quebecers benefit from Hydro-Québec's export sales? The utility claims that profits from these sales allow it to keep rates low in Quebec. Its critics doubt it will make any profit on exports of power from the Great Whale complex; that they strongly doubt that profit can be made with power from the NBR complex, which will cost even more to produce. Critics accuse Hydro-Québec of selling cheap in order to increase its market share, and to earn the American currency it needs to repay its debts. "We never sell at a discount," says Jacques Guevremont. "If the going price does not yield a sufficient return on our investment we simply don't sell."[12] As with all Hydro-Québec's claims, these cannot be verified, for Hydro-Québec refuses to make public the detailed economic studies which justify its decisions, saying that to do so would give advantage to competitors and clients.

Yet it is in order to generate power for export sales and for industrial use in Quebec that the Great Whale complex is being developed. Most of the growth in demand that Hydro-Québec anticipates, and that, it says, make this project necessary, it attributes not to factors such as increases in Quebec's population or increased use of electricity in homes, but to growth in industrial demand and in export commitments.

To create benefits for a subset of Quebec society — which happens to include the proponents of James Bay II — Hydro-Québec, borrowing on the collective credit of Quebecers, will go deeply into debt. At the end of 1990, Hydro-Québec owed almost $26-billion. During the 1990s it plans to borrow more than $40-billion — more than almost any other company in Canada. By the end of the decade, its total debt will have risen to about

$65-billion — that is roughly $8,500 per Quebecer. Hydro-Québec claims that its debt differs from other kinds of public debt. It is in business, it points out, and it is in good financial health; it borrows money to pay for the facilities with which it generates the electricity it sells, making a profit and servicing its debt.

The criteria by which its financial health is measured, however, are designed not to assure the interests of the people of Quebec, but those of the money lenders. One of these criteria, for instance, is that Hydro-Québec earn enough in a year to pay the interest on its debt. This assures the lenders a steady stream of return on their investment. But the standards of financial prudence that apply to ordinary people — such as the rule that one does not take out a mortgage whose service requires more than 30 percent of one's income — do not apply to Hydro-Québec. Though it spends as much as half of its income servicing its debt, it can and does continue to borrow, and thus to increase its total debt.

In Quebec the level of total public debt, about one-fifth of which is contributed by Hydro-Québec, is among the highest in the world (as is the level of private debt). Quebecers have a tradition of borrowing for grandiose public projects, and leaving future generations with the bill. An insouciant attitude to debt common here was articulated when it turned out that the 1976 Olympic Games in Montreal were going to cost a billion dollars; the then mayor of Montreal, Jean Drapeau, explained that repaying debt was like filling a bathtub — one just let the tap drip and eventually the tub was filled.

But as Hydro-Québec's tub gets bigger, so must the drips: that is, as the utility begins to feel the strain of servicing the billions borrowed to build the first phase of the James Bay project, it has been raising its rates. Cheap electricity has always been a foundation of Quebec's economy. It has, the economic planners say, given the province's businesses and industries a competitive edge, and benefited ordinary Quebecers by freeing up some discretionary income. Raising rates was politically easy and economically painless when base rates are low. Now they are rising faster than inflation to levels at which they are beginning to hurt Quebecers. To finance the Great Whale complex — and the capital boom from which its proponents will benefit — critics predict that electricity rates for ordinary Quebecers will double over the next decade.

* * *

Electricity — or rather the services into which electric-powered gadgets convert it, such as light, refrigeration, and motor drive, is like an addictive drug; the cheaper it is, the easier it is to become hooked. Quebecers use more electricity per person (and more electricity per unit of economic value produced) than almost any other people in the world. They use so much because they live in a cold country; because they have so many industries that gobble up electricity; and because, since their electricity has been so cheap, they waste it.[13]

There are many ways in which the efficiency of electricity use can be improved — that is, in which the amount of electricity used can be decreased without decreasing the services it delivers. The classic example of efficiency is the compact fluorescent light bulb, which uses less than one-fifth the electric energy of an incandescent bulb, yet provides the same amount of light.

Many power companies, especially in those parts of the United States where electricity is expensive, are investing in what are called demand side measures — programs to improve the efficiency with which their clients use electricity. They are, for example, giving away free, energy-efficient light bulbs; auditing electrical use in buildings; estimating the savings their customers can achieve; and giving rebates or zero-interest loans so customers can buy insulation, windows, weatherstripping, efficient refrigerators and the like.

Energy savings by customers represent, for utilities, a source of energy. Energy analyst Amory Lovins has coined the term "negawatts" for the units of electric power which, because they were saved, the utility did not have to generate. Prodded by people like Lovins, utilities are becoming thrifty shoppers. In the exercise known as least-cost planning, they compare the prices of all the supply resources from which they can deliver energy services to their customers, and invest, first, in the options with least cost. This seemingly common-sense procedure is beginning to revolutionize the power industry, for negawatts (and other alternative supply resources such as independent power producers and co-generators) are usually much cheaper (in direct cost to the utility, and in overall cost to society) than megawatts. According to Lovins, in the 1980s, the United States has been getting seven times more new energy from savings as from net increases in supply.[14]

The benefits of efficiency programs for everybody are striking. Hydro-Québec can buy negawatts for less than megawatts from the Great Whale complex. New York and Vermont can buy negawatts for less than megawatts imported from Quebec. Investments in negawatts create more jobs and better stimulate local economies than do investments in energy supply. In Quebec, demand side measures programs create about four times more jobs per dollar than do investments in hydroelectric dams.[15] These jobs are created in the hardware stores, lumber-yards, window factories, and small construction companies near where most people live, not at dam sites in northern Quebec, and the skills they require better match the mix of skills in the work force than do those required on hydroelectric projects. Plugging energy leaks also plugs cash leaks. Unlike money spent on dams, which is concentrated within narrow sectors of the economy, money spent on efficiency programs is widely distributed, and tends to circulate within communities, from, say, worker to restaurant to clothes store — longer than does money spent on dams. This effect is magnified by the fact that, as consumers' electricity bills go down because of increased efficiency, people have more cash to spend on other things, and tend to spend locally.

Similarly, in Vermont and New York, investments in efficiency programs create three to four times more jobs per dollar than investments in imports from Quebec, and where imports drain money from regional economies, efficiency programs keep money in local circulation.

Efficiency programs have other advantages relative to big supply increases. They increase a utility's flexibility. Since it takes the best part of a decade to build a hydroelectric complex, Hydro-Québec is planning to make multibillion dollar commitments based on forecasts fraught with uncertainty. A lot — public opinion, prices, interest rates, technology, government regulations — can change in a decade. But once committed to building its megaproject (and once locked into firm, long-term export deals) Hydro-Québec cannot adjust to such changes. By postponing such risky commitments, efficiency programs buy time, and increase the resilience of the energy system.

Finally, efficiency programs do negligible damage to the environment.

For these reasons, the opponents of James Bay II say that Hydro-Québec should not build dams but save energy. Hydro-Québec claims that it has been helping its customers use energy more efficiently.[16] In 1990, when it announced a massive program of construction for the coming decade, it also announced an efficiency program. The utility estimates that by 1999 it could stimulate energy savings of 23 terawatthours a year by stimulating its customers to use existing efficient technologies at a cost, to the utility, less than the cost of getting that energy by building dams. By investing almost $2-billion during the decade in demand side measures such as discounts on light bulbs and hot water tank insulators, questionnaires and tips to residential customers, energy audits of industrial customers, and subsidies to industries to switch to efficient motors, the utility plans to realize only about half these potential savings.

It will reduce its load by about one-tenth of what it would be without conservation. The amount it will be saving every year at the end of the decade will equal the annual consumption of the city of Montreal, or the annual production of the Great Whale complex.

Hydro-Québec and its political masters insist that despite its conservation efforts its load will grow, and that it has no choice but to build more dams. Lise Bacon, Quebec's current Minister of Energy and Bourassa's right hand woman, has declared that "reducing our energy consumption here and there will not save us enough energy. We'll never have enough energy without [James Bay II]. We're already three years late [in starting construction] and it's almost too late. Do we want to be lighting our houses by candlelight in 1998? That's what we have to think about."

Hydro-Québec's critics say its conservation efforts are puny; less than the other two major electric utilities in Canada, Ontario Hydro and B.C. Hydro, and a good deal less than many American utilities. Hydro-Québec is only spending on conservation about one-twentieth of what it is spending on dams. They complain that Hydro-Québec is skimming the cream off the conservation potential, and that not taking optimal efficiency measures now makes it impossible to do so later. They accuse Hydro-Québec of paying lip-service to conservation, of only doing enough to soften up the public opposition so as to facilitate the construction of dams.

Talk of more conservation is unrealistic, Hydro-Québec says. Its critics disagree. Ian Goodman has estimated that, using existing technology, at least 27 terawatthours of electric energy could be saved in Quebec every year by the end of the 1990s — more than twice what Hydro-Québec plans to be saving, and more than it estimates it could save — at a cost less than that of building new dams. Investing in this saving would defer the need to build the Great Whale complex until the year 2015, while allowing Hydro-Québec to continue to meet its commitments on the domestic and export markets. He suggests, in fact, that aggressive conservation could stop Hydro-Québec's load growing at all during the first two decades of the next century. As well as efficiency measures, Quebec could get, some estimate, as much as four times the power output of the Great Whale complex from co-generators, such as the province's many pulp and paper mills, which have surplus heat and steam, as well as from small independent hydroelectric plants. Hydro-Québec discourages such developments by offering paltry payment for power fed into its grid by private producers.

There is so much electricity to be saved in Quebec, and the cost of saving much of it is so low that, as a number of analysts have suggested, Hydro-Québec could actually export power freed up by efficiency measures. Quebecers' total electricity bills would be reduced; Hydro-Québec would profit; importing utilities would get power for less than if they generated it themselves; and no dams would be built.

As a supplier of electricity, Hydro-Québec is extraordinarily efficient. Unlike electric power systems that rely on burning fuel, in hydroelectric systems almost all of the energy harnessed is conserved in the chain of conversions that deliver services to consumers. Why does Hydro-Québec not do more about improving the efficiency with which electricity is used? "We can't force people to lower the temperature." Jacques Guevremont has explained. "We're not all powerful. We can't choose light bulbs for them. Let us be realistic. We're not dictators. Our duty is to service. We'll supply electricity to whoever wants to plug into our system. The consumer is king."[17]

But to suggest that demand is fate, that Hydro-Québec's customers autonomously create its growing load, is false. The utility has aggressively boosted demand by promoting consumption, notably by means of subsidies to and risk-sharing deals with energy-glutton industries.

Another reason why Hydro-Québec does not engineer a serious reduction in its demand is that to recover the cost of doing so, the utility would have to raise electricity rates. But for consumers who participate in efficiency programs, the increase in rates would be more than offset by the reduction in power consumption; their monthly electric bills would go down, which is all they really care about. To argue that programs should not be launched because they are unfair to consumers who do not participate in them yet suffer rate increases caused by them, is specious; there are many ways of making things fair for everybody.

One of the real reasons why Hydro-Québec does not do more about efficiency is, I think, its corporate culture, which finds everything about demand side measures antipathetic. The utility has some of the best hydraulic engineers in the world. They like dealing with dams, which are hard and quantifiable and controllable. They like working on big, prestigious construction projects, and working with their peers in other large corporations. When it comes to designing public information campaigns, to persuading millions of people to use such modest technologies as low-flow shower heads and insulation, Hydro-Québec's engineers are unenthusiastic. Another reason for the lack of interest in demand side measures, I think, is that they would cut off benefits which will flow to the proponents of James Bay II.

The advocates of efficiency see that, eventually, waste will have to be curtailed, and they want it curtailed now, before more damage is done, before all the wild rivers are gone. They have found a dynamic vehicle for their ideas in the fight to stop James Bay II; the environmentalists and Native rights activists have found, in the arguments for efficiency, powerful new arguments integrating and furthering their causes. A character in a novel Amory Lovins co-authored says that the energy policies he favours are neither left nor right, politically, but in front.[18] Natives once used anti-colonial rhetoric in their struggles, and environmentalists used anti-development rhetoric in theirs. Now both are speaking in the resolutely market-oriented language of least-cost planning, and winning political ground. There is a fine irony in the fact that the Native people, once perceived as backward, should now be advocating advanced ways of running the energy business, while Hydro-Québec's technocrats should be seen as primitive. "When I go to Quebec," says Lovins, "I feel like I'm in some valley full of strange critters that everybody thought was extinct."[19]

NOTES

1. Alternative spellings are Kuutjuaraapik, and Whapmagoostoo or Whapmag'stui. The twin villages, referred to as Great Whale River in English, are known in French as Poste-de-la-Baleine (whaling station).

2. National Energy Board, Hearing Orders No EH-3-89 and AO-1-EH-3-89, Hydro-Québec Applications to Export Electricity to the New York Power Authority and Vermont Joint Owners, Panel No 1 of the Grand Council of the Crees (of Québec), Policy and Position of the Grand Council of the Crees (of Québec), Testimony of John Petagumscum, Sr., Submitted on February 14, 1990.

3. "As It Happens" CBC Radio, 6 June 1991; Catherine Leconte, "L'entrevue du lundi: Matthew Coon-Come," Le Devoir (Montreal), 23 September 1991; see also Wittenborn, James Bay Project.

4. National Energy Board. Hearing Orders No EH-3-89 and AO-1-EH-3-89. Hydro-Québec Applications to Export Electricity to the New York Power Authority and Vermont Joint Owners. Panel No 1 of the Grand Council of the Crees (of Québec). Testimony of Grand Chief Matthew Coon-Come. Submitted on February 14, 1990; The Toronto Globe and Mail, 31 August 1991; Address to a forum, sponsored by the Canadian Nature Federation, on Hydroelectricity Developments and Energy Policy in the Province of Quebec, Montreal, 1 February 1990.

5. To avoid the Great Whale hydroelectric project, which they knew was on the drawing board, and in order to establish an all-Inuit community, about half of the Inuit of Kuujuarapik moved some 260 kilometres north in 1983 to a new village, Umiujiak.

6. See, for instance, Hélène Lajambe, "D'une baie James à l'autre," La Presse (Montreal), 23 March 1987.

7. One of the concerns animating opposition to power lines is the risk that the electromagnetic fields that surround them cause cancer and other health problems. Such fields can make physical changes to living cells. To determine whether they

affect health requires comparison of the health of a group of exposed people to the health of another group, a so-called control group, that was not exposed. Finding such a control group is difficult, since we are all bathed by electromagnetic fields. Hydro-Québec, and other electric utilities, assures us that their studies suggest no harmful effects are occurring. Other people say that the question remains unresolved, but that prudence dictates avoiding exposure to such fields, especially when it is easy to do so.

8. Bruce Aikman, interview with author, 13 July 1984.

9. Picard, "James Bay," 17 April 1990.

10. Ian Goodman and W.B. Marcus, Manitoba Hydro Submission in Respect to Major Capital Projects, Joint Testimony to Manitoba Public Utilities Board on behalf of Concerned Citizens of Manitoba, Sierra Club of Western Canada, Manitoba Branch, and Conservation Strategy Association of Manitoba. Revised, September 1990.

11. Bélanger, Gérard and Bernard, Jean-Thomas, "Hydro-Quebec et les alumineries," Le Devoir (Montreal), 20 October 1989; The Montreal Gazette, 10 November 1990.

12. Jean-Marc Carpentier, "Electricity exports in a context of complementarity," Forces 89 (Spring 1990): 40-42.

13. Electricity has been cheap in Canada not only because of nature's generosity in endowing the country with water power, but also because of governments' generosity to utilities. Provincial governments in Canada give their electric utilities benefits, such as water rights, debt guarantees, tax exemptions, and permission to degrade the natural environment, for which the utilities pay little if at all. Such disguised subsidies lower the price of electricity, and encourage overconsumption.

14. E The Environmental Magazine, May/June 1991.

15. See National Energy Board, Hearing Orders No EH-3-89 and AO-1-EH-3-89. Hydro-Québec Applications to Export Electricity to the New York Power Authority and Vermont Joint Owners. Panel No 3 of the Grand Council of the Crees (of Québec). Economic and Technical Aspects and Electricity Demand in Quebec. Testimony of William B. Marcus and Ian Goodman. Submitted February 20, 1990.

16. As it indeed it has, but surely not by means of the baffling message of the ad it was running until the 1990s, which announced that "at Hydro-Québec, electrifficiency is looking after your safety with energy and heart," and showed happy people using gleaming electrical appliances.

17. Jacques Guevremont, testimony before National Energy Board, Montreal, 22 February 1990.

18. Lovins, Energy Unbound.

19. Paul Wells, "Most utilities must prove their proposal is cheapest," The Montreal Gazette, 24 July 1991.

CHAPTER 10

Struggle

The conflict now taking place over the James Bay project is, fundamentally, about power. It is a struggle between groups with irreconcilable visions of the world — the bulldozer coalition and the efficiency coalition — for power to choose the technology that will shape the future. It is also a struggle for power between two tribes, the Crees and the Québécois, each seeing itself as a victim and each seeing the other as barring the path to autonomy.

Though the Crees have threatened to lie down in front of trucks, blockade roads, occupy substations, topple transmission lines, and shoot at helicopters, there has, as yet, been no such direct action. The methods the Crees and their allies are using to stop James Bay II are verbal. In Quebec, in the northeastern states, and in Europe, they are arguing wherever they can find a forum — before regulatory bodies, before environmental impact review panels, before courts, before legislative body hearings, before voters, on the streets, in the news media, and more. Their strategy has been to try to get Hydro-Québec's most recent export contracts with Vermont and with New York state canceled, to tie up the hydroelectric project in the courts, and to win the hearts and minds of the public to their cause.

The proponents, too, are arguing and manoeuvring. Their strategy has been to present the public, where possible, with a *fait accompli*, with a project to which so much has been committed that it cannot be altered or stopped, and to limit debate by withholding information, by refusing to discuss fundamental questions, and by entangling all tribunals in jurisdictional squabbles between Ottawa and Quebec.

For decades now, critics in Quebec have been calling for a debate on energy, for some tribunal within which hydroelectric projects, their justification, cost, potential impacts, and alternatives can be scrutinized. There is, as yet, no such tribunal. There exists, for instance, no regulatory body through which Hydro-Québec has to account to the public of Quebec — who, after all, own the utility as well as the natural resources it exploits, and are the guarantors of its debt. There are no representatives of consumers on Hydro-Québec's board of directors. Through the electoral process, the public has a token measure of control over Hydro-Québec; the elected provincial government appoints the head (or, currently, the co-heads) of the utility, and a parliamentary commission, which now meets once every three years, traditionally ratifies Hydro-Québec's plans without much fuss. Hydro-Québec, the principal proponent of James Bay II, is an oligarchy.

Québécois have tolerated this in part because, like all Canadians, they are generally readier to be governed than are Americans, and in part because they have seen Hydro-Québec as the incarnation of their national aspirations, and the agent for fulfilling them. The Québécois, as one put it to me, *prennent pour du cash* (take as gospel) Hydro-Québec's words.

Hydro-Québec's publicists have told them that Quebec's rivers are running with "white gold," an almost magical source of wealth, which heroic engineers and workers subdued by building cathedrals in James Bay.

The first major clash over the Great Whale project occurred in February 1990, when both Hydro-Québec, and the Crees, their advisers, and opposition groups from both Quebec and the States, testified at public hearings before Canada's National Energy Board on Hydro-Québec's request for a licence to export power to Vermont and to New York. The National Energy Board, the federal body that regulates electricity exports, serves as a forum for Canadian utilities to settle differences that arise from their mutual competition for slices of the same pie, the electricity market of the Northeast. Its rules severely limit the content of debate; it is hopelessly inadequate as a forum for dealing with the dispute over James Bay II. The proponents' arguments persuaded the Board to issue the licences requested — as it almost invariably does —but the opponents' arguments persuaded it to attach an unusual requirement — that the federal government review the environmental impacts of the Great Whale project before construction began. Rankled by this constraint, Hydro-Québec appealed the decision in the Federal Court of Canada, arguing that only Quebec has jurisdiction over how electricity is generated in the province. Hydro-Québec won its case; the environmental condition was lifted.

This pattern of inadequate forums, limited debate, and jurisdictional tangles is even more evident in the realm of environmental impact review. The James Bay and Northern Québec Agreement established two regimes for reviewing environmental and social impacts of developments, one in the Cree homelands, between the 49th and 55th parallels, and the second in the Inuit homelands, north of the 55th parallel. In each area there are two joint government-Native committees, one for questions falling in federal jurisdiction, and the other for questions of provincial jurisdiction.[1] Alan Penn, who helped develop these procedures, points out that the Agreement fails to draw boundaries between provincial and federal jurisdiction. The result is "a no man's land, within which the strongest voice carries the day."[2] The strongest voice has been Quebec's.

Ottawa wants to avoid antagonizing Quebec, with which it is engaged in yet another round of negotiations as to how powers should be divided within Canada, and nothing would antagonize Quebec more than a confrontation over hydro-electric projects, the symbol and seat of economic power in the province. The federal government, therefore, claiming that natural resources were solely a provincial responsibility, reneged on the promises it made in the James Bay and Northern Québec Agreement to participate in environmental impact reviews in the James Bay area. Only the provincial-Native regimes would apply.

In June 1989, court decisions on dam projects in Alberta and Saskatchewan confirmed that the federal government, quite independently of promises it had made in the James Bay and Northern Québec Agreement and broken, had a legal responsibility to apply its own process of reviewing environmental impacts to the Great Whale complex because this project would affect migratory bird breeding habitat, fisheries, navigable waterways, and other areas of federal jurisdiction. Bureaucrats in Ottawa and Quebec repeatedly tried and failed to negotiate a joint federal-provincial review.

In November 1990, eager to get construction under way, Hydro-Québec decided to split the Great Whale project into two parts, first the roads, airports and other infrastructure, and then the dams and dikes and transmission lines, and to present the first part of the project for immediate environmental review to the provincial-Native committees. This, the Crees charged, made no sense, except as an attempt to limit debate on the hydroelectric project itself — to prepare for which was the sole purpose of the infrastructure. Even Quebec's environment minister, Pierre

Paradis, argued for a single comprehensive review of the Great Whale complex. But his department is young, small, poor and politically weak, and he lost this argument with the energy minister, Lise Bacon. The federal government went along with the split; it agreed to suspend its laws, and not to review the impacts of the infrastructure but only those of the dams.

Early in 1991, hoping to begin construction in the fall, Hydro-Québec delivered its study of the environmental impact of the roads and access infrastructure for the Great Whale project to the provincial-Cree environmental review committee and gave it 45 days to review it. According to Alan Penn, the Crees' representative on this committee, the material was stale — a patchwork of studies done in the 1970s — and reflected a cynically dismissive attitude to social issues. The Crees refused to participate in what they considered a token process of ratification. In June 1991, Crees blocked members of the Inuit-provincial committee from leaving the Great Whale airport to hold a hearing in Kuujjuarapik. In September 1991, a federal court may have ended the shenanigans and the impasse when it agreed with the Crees that the federal process of environmental review described in the James Bay and Northern Québec Agreement should be implemented. If this decision is upheld on appeal it would represent a victory for the Crees. Holding proper hearings would delay the start of construction for at least two more years. The hearings could lead to an adequate tribunal for presenting their case and attacking the proponents' case. And a decision not to approve the hydroelectric project would be a decision of the federal government, not just a recommendation (as would be the case if the hearings were held under the federal government's environmental assessment review process.)

The Crees say they will participate in a global federal-provincial-Cree review of the Great Whale project under the terms of the James Bay and Northern Québec Agreement, if they are given $12.6-million — 0.01 percent of the estimated costs of the Great Whale complex — to research their case and hire experts. They insist that the questions to be addressed at the review include the justification for the project and a comparison of its costs and impacts to that of alternatives such as efficiency, and they insist that Hydro-Québec release to the public information about its construction costs, and about its revenue from exports and from energy-hungry industries.

To many people, and especially to Americans, these sound like demands for fair play. Environmental impact reviews are battles in which Hydro-Québec has the heavy artillery. Hydro-Québec's environmental department has several hundred staff, and spends more than $30-million every year. The data it collects and presents in its voluminous reports are, according to Alan Penn, "not designed to focus on problems, but to provide general reassurance."[3] To hear the views of all sides requires funding the other sides, and doing so is normal practice in many polities, including Ontario and the United States. Furthermore, it is now accepted as being fair and prudent to require a utility to justify its choices and prove that they are the least-cost options.

Lise Bacon has explicitly said that her government would not fund the Crees so they could oppose it through environmental tribunes. In Quebec, members of environmental review committees do not get to set the questions which Hydro-Québec must answer. They are like people judging a job candidate on the basis of her answers to her own questions. The only questions the hydroelectric-industrial complex in Quebec is willing to entertain in the environmental impact assessment process — or anywhere else for that matter — are those concerning ways of attenuating the impacts of development. Questions of the basic design, wisdom, or fairness of a project are not to be debated. Thus the aluminum industry — whose industrial plants are exempt from public environmental impact hearings — complains that in general such hearings "degenerate into a philosophical debate on the future of the planet."[4] Questions of the James Bay project's *raison d'être* are not to be discussed, say its proponents, because the Natives, in signing the James Bay and Northern Québec Agreement, have agreed that it should be built, have accepted compensation for it, and have promised not to oppose it. Shortly before the engineering firms Lavalin and SNC fused, for example, they jointly took out half-page newspaper advertisements in which they reminded Quebecers of the promise the Native people had made. "It is our opinion," the firms said, "that one must avoid letting Quebec become the territory where the procedure for approval of projects is used for ends other than the protection of the environment and the evaluation of the quality of the projects."

For the developers, environmental impact review has been, basically, a "procedure for the approval of projects." For the Crees and their allies it could become a way of blocking the project. For both parties the function of environmental impact reviews is essentially political.

In their attempts to block the Great Whale project, the Crees and their allies are engaged in more than a dozen legal actions, mainly in Canada but also in the United States. In April 1990, the Crees launched the central battle in their legal war, a case requesting a permanent injunction on the construction of the Great Whale project. Even though they explicitly renounced their aboriginal rights in the James Bay and Northern Québec Agreement, they argue, these rights were not extinguished, and they still own both the land and the resources of much of northern Quebec. This case is due to be heard in April 1992.

In the spring of 1991 the Crees fought to get Hydro-Québec, and the 13 multinational companies with which it had signed risk-sharing contracts, to reveal details of these contracts. The refusal of the companies to do so — they obtained a court injunction banning publication within Quebec of one leaked contract, a futile gesture since it was freely reported outside the province — served to expose Hydro-Québec's secretiveness to the unflattering light of publicity, and to question its wisdom and credibility. Hydro-Québec insisted that the secrecy was necessary to

protect its clients' competitiveness; in fact, aluminum companies in almost every other part of the world freely reveal to their competitors the
rates they pay for electricity. The real reason for keeping the contracts
secret was, probably, that the contracts hid subsidies, and under the terms
of its free trade agreement with Canada, the United States can slap duty
on imports of subsidized products.

The contracts tied the price paid for electricity to the price the clients
obtain for their product, such as aluminum. With the price for aluminum
down, some of the companies were buying electricity for half of what it
cost Hydro-Québec to produce it. The critics claimed that Hydro-Québec
was losing money on these sales, and that the only justification for building the Great Whale project was to meet the demand created by these
sales — together the 13 contracts account for a quantity of power almost
equal to that which the Great Whale complex would generate — and by
exporting power to America.

* * *

Early in 1990, Denny Alsop, an American who had canoed on the
Eastmain River before it was dammed, suggested to the Crees the idea for
a public relations campaign in the Northeast. Crees and Inuit, people
between whom relations were traditionally strained, built in the village
of Great Whale a hybrid craft — it had the bow of an Indian canoe, and
the stern of an Inuit kayak — to which they gave a hybrid name —
Odeyak, a combination of the Cree word for canoe and the Inuit word
kayak.

Some 60 Natives, mainly Crees from Whapmagoostui (including John
Petagumscum) and Inuit from Kuujjuarapik, paddled and trucked the
Odeyak through Montreal, down the Hudson River to New York City. On
Earth Day, in April 1990, the Odeyak reached Times Square. Matthew
Coon-Come spoke there. "Hydroelectric development is flooding the

land, destroying wildlife and killing our people," he said, "and eventually we will all be victims."

On that trip, Natives of northern Quebec left their enclave to communicate directly with non-Natives. Southerners met them, in grungy church basements, in Society of Friends' meeting halls, and listened to their message: that North and South were connected, that it was Vermont and New York imports that would trigger construction of the Great Whale project. The proponents of this project "are telling the Americans this is cheap and clean," said Robbie Dick, the chief of the Whapmagoostui band. "But it's not cheap for us. When you turn on your switch, you're killing us."

By means of the voyage of the Odeyak, the Natives won the hearts of many Americans, excited indignation at the arrogant treatment of nature and Natives, and mobilized their political energies. The main goal of American opposition to James Bay II has been to cancel the Vermont and New York contracts. In Vermont, American grassroots opponents testified before the Vermont Public Service Board, the state's regulatory agency, when it reviewed the contract under which Vermont Joint Owners would import power from Hydro-Québec. The Crees and their advisers testified here too. In October 1990, the board approved the import of 340 megawatts of firm power, but required Hydro-Québec to swear that none of this power would come from new dams in the James Bay area.

The New York contract being a much larger one, the struggle there has been more important. There is no regulatory agency overseeing the New York Power Authority; it answers directly to the Governor of the state, Mario Cuomo. The Sierra Club, PROTECT, the Crees and others took legal action against the New York Power Authority, arguing that the James Bay II projects from which the electricity would come should be subject to New York's environmental standards, which are more stringent than Quebec's. Their suit was not granted. The opponents, however, have been putting political pressure on, among other politicians,

Mayor David Dinkins of New York City, and Governor Mario Cuomo. Much of the power from the import contract is destined for New York City. Though Mayor Dinkins has no authority over electricity imports to the state, he has considerable political influence, and was persuaded — perhaps in part because he is black, and thus sympathetic to the Crees as an ethnic minority — to write to the New York Power Authority requesting a delay in the ratification of the contract. Governor Cuomo is reported to have presidential ambitions, and successful presidential candidates need environmentally clean records. He was persuaded by the environmentalists to exercise his authority. In September 1991, the New York Power Authority announced that it was extending from November 1991 to November 1992 the deadline for ratifying its contract to import 1,000 megawatts of firm power from Hydro-Québec, and Governor Cuomo announced that he had requested an economic and environmental study of the impacts of the contract, a study which will be completed in spring 1992.

Encouraged, the activists in New York continue their campaign. They have testified at hearings before the environmental protection committee of the municipal council of New York City, for instance, where the proposition was debated that the contract be withdrawn until an adequate environmental impact assessment is conducted. They have organized support for a bill by which the New York Senate would prevent the New York Power Authority from buying power from Quebec unless the New York utility conducted a study of the environmental impacts of its purchase. They demonstrate regularly against James Bay II. Groups have been demonstrating during the summer of 1991 by cycling through Vermont and New York; they ended their tours in early October in New York City at a three-day series of benefit concerts, the Ban the Dam Jam.

The success of the movement in the United States opposing James Bay II is not due just to political action, but also to the extent to which demand is being reduced by energy efficiency programs. According to

Ian Goodman, the reduction in New York's energy demand between 1989 and 1991 alone is producing more energy than the state plans to import from Quebec, and at a cheaper price. As well, small independent power companies, some of whom burn natural gas imported from Western Canada, are selling cheap power to New York. Some people question whether New York needs power from Quebec, and whether buying it would make economic sense.

Similarly, utilities in New England are questioning the economic value of their contracts with Hydro-Québec; with the economic recession, and the success of energy efficiency programs, they too have sharply reduced their power needs.

*   *   *

In Quebec, where the fate of the Great Whale River will be decided, the struggle for power between the bulldozer coalition and the Crees grows more polarized and the arguments more strident. The grassroots coalition of opposition groups in Quebec has been attempting to mobilize public opinion in ways similar to those used south of the border. In the summer of 1991, for instance, a group including Natives, environmentalists and trade unionists toured the province to drum up support. Quebecers remain ambivalent and confused. A poll conducted by Hydro-Québec during the summer of 1991 found that 56 percent of Quebecers are in favour of the Great Whale project; at best a slim majority, if this poll reflects reality, and a declining one, since public support for Hydro-Québec was much higher a few years ago.

Shortly after the New York Power Authority announced it was postponing its final decision on the 1,000 megawatts contract, Bourassa announced another year's postponement of the date at which construction of the Great Whale project would start. The proponents continue to insist, with a vehemence bordering on desperation, that the Great Whale project has to be built. "Great Whale is an environmentally acceptable economic necessity," says Lise Bacon, the Minister of Energy. "With or without exports, despite major energy conservation programs, sooner or later, we will need this energy. Great Whale is the least expensive and more environmentally sound way for us to procure it."[5] She refuses to hold a public debate; it has already happened, she says.

Hydro-Québec has mounted an expensive public relations effort aimed particularly at the United States and at Europe. This attempt to restore its image as an environmentally-sensitive corporate citizen is of some importance because, as its image deteriorates, it loses the confidence of the investors from whom it borrows. In media such as its annual reports, beautifully illustrated with photos of unspoiled nature, or of romantic old poles carrying power to snowbound villages, the utility praises itself for its fastidious care of wild nature, and for its concern for human needs. It arrogates the rhetoric of its opponents; its chairman and chief executive officer, Richard Drouin, speaks of sustainable development now, and of "negawatts." In advertisements aimed at Quebecers it plays on fears about the steady supply of electricity.

The proponents are frustrated by what they see as the unrepresentative but hyperactive opposition in the United States, and by the intransigence of the Crees. Both Bourassa and the chief of the Parti Québécois fulminate about tiny minorities getting in the way of the majority of Québécois.

The magnitude of what is at stake has grown with the recent growth of nationalism in Quebec, and with the resurgence of the possibility that Quebec could separate from Canada. Behind the few thousand intransigent Crees, some Quebecers see the manipulative hand of the federal government. If Quebec were to separate, some say, the federal government would support the Cree and Inuit claims to their homelands, and would take back Nouveau-Québec, the northern half of the province, from Quebec, and give it to the Natives. The new nation-state of Quebec would occupy only the old territory of Nouvelle-France, the land France colonized along the Saint Lawrence River.

And what would happen to the James Bay project? Would the federal government take it over? Would the Crees form Hydro-Creebec, and run it themselves? Would it become the economic base of the sovereign nation which the Crees say they will form if Quebec separates, a nation which has no other visible means of support? Or will the threat of losing the James Bay hydroelectric project, which *indépendantistes* see as Quebec's entry card to the planetary club of nation states, be what keeps Quebec in Canada?

NOTES

1. Thus, in the Inuit homelands, there is the federal-Inuit regime, the Kativik Advisory Committee on the Environment, with representatives of both the federal and provincial governments and of the Inuit; and the provincial-Inuit regime, the Kativik Environmental Quality Commission, with Inuit and provincial government representatives. Similarly, in the Cree homelands, there is the federal-Cree committee, the James Bay Advisory Committee on the Environment, with representatives of both the federal and provincial governments and of the Crees; and the provincial-Cree committee, the Environmental and Social Impact Review Committee, with Cree and provincial government representatives.
2. Alan Penn, interview with author, Montreal, 3 June 1983.
3. Gorrie, "The James Bay Power Project."
4. "L'industrie met en cause le sérieux des audiences publiques du BAPE," *Le Devoir* (Montreal), 20 September 1991. (My translation.)
5. Michelle Lalonde, "Soaring price tag raises serious doubts about Great Whale." *The Toronto Globe and Mail*, 30 April 1991.

SELECTED BIBLIOGRAPHY

A great deal has been written on the James Bay project. Of the documents I have consulted I list here those I found most useful in making this book.

Berkes, Fikret. "Some Environmental and Social Impacts of the James Bay Hydroelectric Project, Canada." *Journal of Environmental Management* 12 (1981): 157-172.

Berkes, Fikret. "The Intrinsic Difficulty of Predicting Impacts: Lessons from the James Bay Hydro Project." *Environmental Impact Assessment Review* 8 (1988): 201-220.

Bocking, Richard. *Canada's Water for Sale.* James Lewis and Samuel, 1972.

Boileau, Gilles; Pierre Gangloff; and Camille Laverdière. "Québec: château d'eau surplombant une Amérique assoiffée," *Forces* 7 (1966): 24-37.

Bombardier, Denise. "Guy Coulombe: 25 ans d'étatisme." *L'actualité* (June 1988): 18-22.

Bourassa, Robert. *James Bay.* Harvest House, 1973.

Bourassa, Robert. *Deux fois la Baie James.* Les Éditions La Presse, 1981.

Bourassa, Robert. *Power from the North.* Prentice Hall Canada, 1985.

Brody, Hugh. *Maps and Dreams.* Douglas and McIntyre, 1981.

Brody, Hugh. *Living Arctic; Hunters of the Canadian North.* Douglas and McIntyre, 1987.

Calef, George. *Caribou and the Barren-Lands.* Canadian Arctic Resources Committee and Firefly Books, 1981.

Canadian Arctic Resources Committee, Environmental Committee of Sanikiluaq and Rawson Academy of Science. *Sustainable Development in the Hudson Bay/James Bay Bioregion: An Ecosystem Approach.* Canadian Arctic Resources Committee, 1991.

Chanlat, Alain, with André Bolduc and Daniel Larouche. *Gestion et culture d'entreprise: le cheminement d'Hydro-Québec.* Québec/Amérique, 1984.

Crowe, Keith. *A History of the Original Peoples of Canada.* McGill-Queen's University Press, 1974.

Crowe, Keith. "Claims on the Land." *Arctic Circle* (November/December 1990): 12-23.

Deudney, Daniel. *Rivers of Energy: The Hydropower Potential.* Worldwatch Paper 44 (June 1981).

Diamond, Billy. "Aboriginal Rights: The James Bay Experience." In *The Quest for Justice: Aboriginal Peoples and Aboriginal Rights,* 265-285. Edited by Menno Boldt and J. Anthony Long. University of Toronto Press, 1985.

Diamond, Billy. "Villages of the Dammed: The James Bay Agreement Leaves a Trail of Broken Promises." *Arctic Circle* (November/December 1990): 24-34.

Faucher, Philippe, and Johanne Bergeron. *Hydro-Québec: la société de l'heure de pointe.* Les Presses de l'Université de Montréal, 1986.

Feit, Harvey. "Negotiating Recognition of Aboriginal Rights: History, Strategies and Reactions to the James Bay and Northern Québec Agreement." *Canadian Journal of Anthropology* 1:2 (Winter 1980): 159-171.

Feit, Harvey. "Hunting and the Quest for Power: The James Bay Cree and Whitemen in the Twentieth Century." In *Native Peoples: The Canadian Experience,* edited by R. Bruce Morrison and C. Roderick Wilson, 171-207. McClelland and Steward, 1986.

Francis, Daniel, and Toby Morantz. *Partners in Furs: A History of the Fur Trade in Eastern James Bay, 1600-1870.* McGill-Queen's University Press, 1983.

Fraser, Graham. *PQ; René Lévesque and the Parti Québécois in Power.* Macmillan of Canada, 1984.

Gorrie, Peter. "The James Bay Power Project." *Canadian Geographic* (February/March, 1990): 21-31.

Hadekel, Peter. "Power Politics." *Saturday Night* (June 1984): 15-27.

Hafsi, Taïeb, and Christine Demers. *Le changement radical dans les organisations complexes: le cas d'Hydro-Québec.* Gaëtan Morin, 1989.

Hare, Kenneth and Morley K. Thomas. *Climate Canada.* John Wiley, 1979.

Hazell, Stephen. "Battling Hydro; Taming Quebec's Runaway Corporate Beast is a Herculean Task." *Arctic Circle* (July/August 1991): 40-41.

Hecky, Robert. "Methylmercury Contamination in Northern Canada." *Northern Perspectives* (October 1987): 8-9.

Hughes, Thomas P. *Networks of Power: Electrification in Western Society, 1880-1930.* Johns Hopkins University Press, 1923.

Hogue, Clarence; André Bolduc; and Daniel Larouche. *Québec, un siècle d'électricité.* Libre expression, 1979.

Hydro-Québec. *Hydro-Québec. Des premiers défis à l'aube de l'an 2000.* Forces/Libre expression, 1984.

Hydro-Québec. *Hydro-Québec and the Environment, Hydro-Québec Development Plan 1989-1991 — Horizon 1998.* Hydro-Québec, 1989.

Hydro-Québec. *James Bay: Development, Environment and the Native People of Quebec.* Hydro-Québec, 1989.

Irwin, Colin. "Lords of the Arctic: Wards of the State." *Northern Perspectives* (January-March, 1989): 2-20.

Jacobs, Jane. *The Question of Separatism; Quebec and the Struggle over Sovereignty.* Random House, 1980.

"James Bay: The Wind that Keeps on Blowing." *The Nature of Things.* Canadian Broadcasting Corporation, 1991. (Film.)

Jobin, Carol. *Les enjeux économiques de la nationalisation de l'électricité (1962-1963).* Les Éditions cooperatives Albert St.-Martin, 1978.

Lacasse, Roger. *Baie James, une épopée*. Libre expression, 1983.

Leconte, Catherine. "L'accord source de tous les désaccords." *Le Devoir* (Montreal), 18 September 1991, B1.

Lévesque, René. *Memoirs*. Translated by Philip Stratford. McClelland and Stewart, 1986.

Lovins, Amory; L. Hunter Lovins; and Seth Zuckerman. *Energy Unbound; A Fable for America's Future*. Sierra Club Books, 1986.

MacGregor, Roy. *Chief; The Fearless Vision of Billy Diamond*. Viking, 1989.

Malouf, Justice Albert. *La Baie James indienne: texte intégral du jugement du juge Albert Malouf*. Éditions du jour, 1973.

McKenna, Barrie. "James Bay plan: A Whale for the killing?" *The Toronto Globe and Mail*, 28 September 1991, B18.

Morisset, Jean. *L'identité usurpée*. Vol. 1—*L'Amérique écartée*. Nouvelle optique, 1985.

Munson, Richard. *The Power Makers: The Inside Story of America's Biggest Business...and its Struggle to Control Tomorrow's Electricity*. Rodale Press, 1985.

Penn, Alan. "Development of James Bay: the role of environmental assessment in determining the legal rights to an interlocutory injunction." *Journal of the Fisheries Research Board of Canada* 32 (1975): 136-160.

Penn, Alan. *Background papers on the Hydro-Quebec Development Plan, 1989-1991, Horizon 1998, Environmental Impact Assessment in the James Bay Territory, and Forest Management Issues Related to the Implementation in James Bay of the Forest Act*. A document prepared for the Special General Assembly of the James Bay Crees on hydro-electric and forestry development in the James Bay territory, March 14, 15 and 16, 1989.

Picard, André. "James Bay: A Power Play." *The Toronto Globe and Mail*, 13, 14, 16, and 17 April 1990.

Richardson, Boyce. *James Bay: The plot to drown the North Woods*. Sierra Club, 1972.

Richardson, Boyce. *Strangers Devour the Land: The Cree hunters of the James Bay area versus Premier Bourassa and the James Bay Development Corporation*, Macmillan of Canada, 1975/1991.

Rosenthal, Joyce, and Jan Beyea. *Long-Term Threats to Canada's James Bay From Human Development*. Environmental Policy Analysis Department Report #29, National Audubon Society, New York (July 1989).

Salisbury, Richard. *A Homeland for the Cree: Regional Development in James Bay, 1971-1981*. McGill-Queen's University Press, 1986.

Simard, Jean-Jacques. "Contrepoint: Une perspective québécoise du développement nordique." *Northern Perspectives* (March/April 1988): 22-32.

Smith, Philip. *Brinco: The Story of Churchill Falls*. McClelland and Steward, 1975.

Société d'énergie de la Baie James. *Le Complexe hydroélectrique de La Grande Rivière: réalisation de la première phase*. Les Éditions de la Chenelière, 1987.

Société d'énergie de la Baie James. *Le défi environnement au Complexe hydroélectrique de La Grande Rivière*. Les Éditions de la Chenelière, 1987.

Speck, Frank. *Nascapi: The Savage Hunters of the Labrador Peninsula*. University of Oklahoma Press (1935/1977).

Spence, John, and Gillian Spence. *Ecological Considerations of the James Bay Project*. Montreal, 1972.

Tanner, Adrian. *Bringing Home Animals: Religious Ideology and Mode of Production of the Mistassini Cree Hunters*. Memorial University of Newfoundland, Institute of Social and Economic Research, Social and Economic Studies No. 23, 1979.

Willis, Jane. *Geniesh: An Indian Girlhood*. new press, 1973.

Wittenborn, R., and C. Biegert, eds. *James Bay Project: A River Drowned by Water*. Montreal Museum of Fine Art, 1981.

Wyatt, Alan. *Electric Power: Challenges and Choices*. The Book Press, 1986.

THE MYTH OF THE MARKET

Promises and Illusions

by Jeremy Seabrook

If it had been the purpose of human activity on earth to bring the planet to the edge of ruin, no more efficient mechanism could have been invented than the market economy. Yet the majority of people, especially in the West, place their hope and faith in the mechanism of the market as the bearer of promise for the future.

This promise, to deliver an ever-increasing supply of consumer goods, hides a dark reality: the spreading of market values is leading to social disintegration in the West, and to the destruction of the indigenous cultures in the Third World.

Jeremy Seabrook argues that, if the rhetoric about a sustainable society is to be translated into practical politics, citizens must stand up and resist the growing totalitarian nature of the market, with a passion and energy equal to that of the market system itself.

Educated at Cambridge University and the London School of Economics, Jeremy Seabrook has been a teacher, lecturer, and social worker, as well as a well-known writer and journalist. He contributes regularly to *New Society, The Guardian,* and *The Independent.*

200 pages
Paperback ISBN: 1-895431-08-5 $18.95
Hardcover ISBN: 1-895431-09-3 $37.95
Ecology/Economics

THE NEW WORLD ORDER AND THE THIRD WORLD

edited by DAVE BROAD and LORI FOSTER

The Chinese word for 'crisis' can also be translated as 'opportunity'. Some say the crises of the First and Second World Wars was the opportunity for the Soviet and Chinese revolutions. And in the present crisis, what opportunities, if any, exist? What are the prospects for world peace, for democracy, for social justice? What are the consequences for the Third World, when the whole world is undergoing such dramatic change?

To answer these questions and others, a group of international experts probe the problems and the hopes of some southern hemisphere countries where anti-imperialist struggle is seen as the only opportunity left.

Ed Herman provides the background with an overview of the various assaults that have taken place against national liberation movements by the United States since the early years of this century. Thomas Bodenheimer and Robert Gould examine United States foreign policy in detail since World War II. Susanne Jonas looks at the effect that global political changes have had on Central America. Dave Close discusses the 1990 electorial defeat of the Sandinistas in Nicaragua. Doug Booker describes the role of the fundamentalist churches, especially in the Phillipines. And Dave Broad lays out the historical context of the current international situation as he analyzes the Gulf War and its aftermath.

This work is an up to date, indispensable resource drawn from the experiences of internationally recognized authors so that all of us might better understand world events and their affects in these particularly unpredictable times.

250 pages
Paperback ISBN: 1-895431-16-6   **$19.95**
Hardcover ISBN: 1-895431-17-4   **$38.95**

New From Murray Bookchin —
pioneer thinker, writer, and activist

Bookchin has been involved in the environmental movement for more than thirty years and widely regarded by the international community as one whose ideas are decades ahead of his time. He is a teacher, lecturer, and keynote speaker throughout Europe and North America, and Professor Emeritus at the School of Environmental Studies, Ramapo College of New Jersey and Director Emeritus of the Institute for Social Ecology at Plainfield, Vermont, as well as author of more than a dozen major books, including The Ecology of Freedom, Remaking Society, Toward an Ecological Society, The Philosophy of Social Ecology, *and* The Limits of the City—*all available from* **Black Rose Books.**

URBANIZATION WITHOUT CITIES
The Rise and Decline of Citizenship
revised edition

In this original work, Murray Bookchin introduces provocative ideas about the nature of community, and what it means to be a fully empowered citizen. He believes that the tension that exists between rural and urban society can be a vital source of human creativity, thereby defining a new, richly imaginative politics which can help us recover the power of the individual, restore the positive values and quality of urban life, and reclaim the ideal of the city as a major creative force in our civilization.

340 pages
Paperback ISBN: 1-895431-00-X   **$19.95**
Urban Sociology/History

THE ECOLOGY OF FREEDOM
The Emergence and Dissolution of Hierarchy
Revised edition

The Ecology of Freedom *is a confirmation of his [Bookchin's] status as a penetrating critic not only of the ways in which humankind is destroying itself, but of the ethical imperative to live a better life.*
The Village Voice

The ideas in this book are structured around contrasts between preliterate, non-hierarchical societies—their out-looks, technics, and forms of thinking—and the sweeping changes 'civilization' introduced to the human condition based on hierarchy and domination.

This 1991 edition includes a substantial new introduction which situates the new debates and problems in the ecology movement.

395 pages
Paperback ISBN: 0-921689-72-1   **$19.95**
Hardcover ISBN: 0-921689-73-X   **$38.95**
Ecology

DEFENDING THE EARTH
Debate between Murray Bookchin and Dave Foreman
Introduction by David Levine

"The Great Debate" is what environmental activists called this first public meeting between Bookchin and Foreman, and as expected, sparks flew.

Over the last few years, the ecology movement has been torn by bitter divisions. One of the most serious, and certainly the one which has received the most play in the media, has been between social ecologists and the "deep" ecologists.

Defending the Earth is the outcome of the first public meeting between social ecologist Murray Bookchin and deep ecology activist Dave Foreman. The result of these discussions is a surprising amount of agreement even though some important differences still exist. These differences need to be explored further, and resolved. To its credit, this book points the way forward. Besides being packed with provocative ideas and insights, it is a model of how best to raise difficult political differences within a movement.

Defending the Earth proves that there are creative opportunities within the radical ecology movement for building alliances and connections across community, issue, race, gender, class and political lines.

120 pages
Paperback ISBN: 0-921689-88-8 $12.95
Hardcover ISBN: 0-921689-89-6 $31.95
Ecology

GREEN POLITICS
Agenda For a Free Society
DIMITRIOS ROUSSOPOULOS

It isn't easy to present the truth about the destruction of the earth without falling into the trap of apocalyptic despair, nor is it easy to challenge current assumptions about progress and what the future holds. This book courageously confronts these issues to suggest that we *can* create a new society that is ecologically sustainable, economically viable and socially just.

Widespread patterns of alienation are obliging us to re-consider both the neglected issues of community and of the individual. *Green Politics* is rooted in the conviction that there is a set of principles from which new and innovative solutions, based on a clear appreciation of our interdependent relationship with the environment, may emerge.

An international survey of various Green political parties is presented, featuring their programmes and progress. The result is a stimulating book that challenges accepted ideas about how the world should be organized and suggests the possibility of a safe and more satisfying future for all of us.

Dimitrios Roussopoulos is an editor, writer and economist. He has written widely on international politics (*The Coming of World War Three*), democracy (*The Case For Participatory Democracy*, with C. George Benello) and social change.

250 pages
Paperback ISBN: 0-921689-74-8 $15.95
Hardcover ISBN: 0-921689-75-6 $35.95
Politics/Ecology/Sociology

BLACK ROSE BOOKS

has also published the following related titles:

THE PHILOSOPHY OF SOCIAL ECOLOGY: Essays on Dialectical Naturalism,
  by Murray Bookchin
REMAKING SOCIETY, *by Murray Bookchin*
TOWARD AN ECOLOGICAL SOCIETY, *by Murray Bookchin*
THE MODERN CRISIS, *by Murray Bookchin*
THE LIMITS OF THE CITY, *by Murray Bookchin*
WOLLASTON: People Resisting Genocide, *by Miles Goldstick*
ECOLOGY AS POLITICS, *by André Gorz*
FED UP! The Food Forces that Make You Fat, Sick, and Poor, *by Brett Silverstein*
GREEN CITIES: Ecologically Sound Approaches to Urban Space, *edited by David Gordon*
NO NUKES: Everyone's Guide to Nuclear Power, *by Anna Gyorgy and Friends*
THE NUCLEAR POWER GAME, *by Ronald Babin*
MUTUAL AID: A Factor of Evolution, by Peter Kropotkin, *Introduction*
  by George Woodcock
THE ANARCHIST MOMENT: Reflections on Culture, Nature and Power, *by John Clark*
BEHIND THE SILICON CURTAIN: The Seductions of Work in a Lonely Era,
  by Dennis Hayes

send for a free catalogue of all our titles
BLACK ROSE BOOKS
P.O. Box 1258
Succ. Place du Parc
Montréal, Québec
H3W 2R3

Printed by
the workers of
Editions Marquis, Montmagny, Québec
for
Black Rose Books Ltd.

0160